Higher Miseducation

A Dissident's Essays on the
Assault against Liberal Learning

Jack Kerwick

Higher Miseducation: A Dissident's Essays on the Assault against Liberal Learning

Other books by Jack Kerwick

The American Offensive: Dispatches from the Front
Misguided Guardians: The Conservative Case against Neoconservatism
Christianity and the World: Essays Philosophical, Historical and Cultural

© 2017 Jack Kerwick All Rights Reserved
Print ISBN 978-1-941071-87-8
ebook ISBN 978-1-941071-88-5

This book is sold subject to the condition that it shall not, by way of trade or otherwise, be lent, resold, hired out or otherwise circulated without the publisher's prior consent in any form of binding or cover other than that in which it is published and without a similar condition including this condition being imposed on the subsequent purchaser.

STAIRWAY PRESS—APACHE JUNCTION

Cover Design by Guy D. Corp
www.GrafixCorp.com

STAIRWAY PRESS

www.StairwayPress.com
1000 West Apache Trail #126
Apache Junction, AZ 88120 USA

Introduction

I AM AN academic dissident.

At 45 years of age and as a doctor of philosophy, I have spent nearly my entire adult life in academia.

Almost 19 years ago, immediately upon obtaining my Master's in philosophy and a full eight years prior to acquiring my Ph.D., I began teaching in my field. Before I would be hired full-time at what is now my home institution, I would spend the next 14 years teaching at a diverse array of colleges and universities, institutions extending over half of the country from Baylor University in the Southwest to Temple University in the Northeast.

These were schools that were small and large, teaching-oriented and research-oriented, public and private, secular and religious. While it would be unjust to neglect the significant differences between them, the truth of the matter is that, in varying degrees and despite the other respects in which they differed from one another, all of these schools were guilty of having capitulated to the political fashions of the times.

Traditionally, a classical liberal arts education was ultimately designed to facilitate the "*disinterested*" pursuit of *truth* and *knowledge*. In other words, two things were taken for granted: (1) Truth and, thus, knowledge were obtainable; and (2) The pursuit of truth and knowledge was an emphatically *non-political* enterprise.

With all too few exceptions, the contemporary university has, in effect, abandoned its traditional mission, for as I attempt to show in the following essays, these two core presuppositions have largely been jettisoned.

Yet even this way of putting the matter sorely understates

the current condition, for there are, conceivably, alternative ways of conceiving the mission of the university that, nevertheless, complement its historical self-conception. I myself have argued in other places for a change in emphasis. However, today's university has substituted a vision of higher education that isn't just different than that of the classical ideal, but antithetical to the latter.

Truth, knowledge, reason, objectivity, fact, logic—all are now viewed basically as smokescreens that are meant to conceal ulterior, non-rational, and often "oppressive" operations of *power*. Karl Marx's philosophy, which treated truth claims as instruments by which the ruling class, the bourgeoisie, strengthened its hegemony over the proletariat, has been adjusted to accommodate the political predilections of Marx's present-day successors so that the classical Marxist's emphasis on *class* has shifted onto race and gender.

Thus, appeals to truth and its concomitant concepts are now repudiated as expressions of racial and gender oppression.

Few people outside of the academy are aware of what they or their children can expect to encounter if and when they enter college. It's for the sake of such people that I compiled this collection of my essays from over the last few years. It is my hope that they will serve as a clarion call of sorts, a warning to the larger public that the "education" for the sake of which far too many parents have remortgaged their homes and legions of students and former students have accrued small fortunes worth of debt has been abandoned in exchange for what can only be described as *training* in a *political ideology*.

The extent to which this change marks a departure from the university's traditional mission can't be overstated.

The idea of the *disinterested* pursuit of truth presupposes and affirms *not* that the quest *can* or *should* be *a*political; it embodies the imperative that the pursuit of truth *must* be apolitical. Nor is it difficult to see why this has to be the case.

Politics, after all, is an eminently practical enterprise in that it is all about making a society's institutional arrangements such that they (ostensibly) serve the "greater" or "common good." What's key in politics is not so much truth as feasibility, that which *works*. Political actors are by definition *partisans*. But a liberal arts education, in stark contrast, is supposed to emancipate those who pursue it from practical and, by implication, political concerns. Students of a liberal arts education, then, are not and cannot be partisans. Or, if you will, they are fellow partisans…of truth.

In closing, it needs to be noted that for as bleak as is the picture of the present academic landscape that the essays in this book promise to paint, I choose to have faith that liberal learning remains not only possible but, at least in some corners of academia—like that which I occupy—a reality. There are academics, including left-wing academics, who are as disturbed by the subversion of the classical ideal of higher learning as am I, and who have been busily laboring to rectify this situation. As the postmodern left reaches new excesses, the number of academic dissidents, I'd like to believe, will continue to swell.

It is to the end of dissenting from the prevailing consensus, of resisting the intellectual straightjacket of its orthodoxies, and, hence, of restoring the ideal of liberal learning to its rightful place that I offer this book.

Jack Kerwick

College Campuses: Intellectual- and Diversity-FREE Zones

I STILL BELIEVE in the ideal of a liberal arts education—even if, in practice, I've become more than a bit disenchanted.

As an undergraduate some 20 years ago majoring in religion and philosophy at Wingate University—a small, Southern Baptist institution in North Carolina—I was fortunate to have been taught by genuinely dedicated teachers who saw to it that their students received the classical education in the liberal arts for which they signed up.

To put this point another way, my professors resisted the temptation—a temptation that's all too common among the professoriate in the contemporary academy—to abuse their vocational privileges by *preaching* to, rather than *teaching*, their students. The classroom, my instructors seemed to realize, was not the proper venue in which to air their political and ideological predilections.

In pursuing my master's degree in philosophy from Baylor University, I became increasingly aware of some of my instructors' political views, but there existed a reasonable degree of intellectual diversity in the department. This latter fact, coupled with my professors' unquestionable commitment to the welfare of their students, made my time at Baylor one of the most enjoyable periods of my life.

Sadly, however, I can't say the same about the sentence I served at Temple University while working on my Ph.D.

To a man and woman, Temple's philosophy department consisted of hard left ideologues. As hard leftists are wont to do, they wore their ideologies on their sleeves. For example, not long after I began my course work, during my second semester, I had a conversation with one of my professors that stopped before it began. Given that my area of specialization is political philosophy, this experience of mine was tremendously disheartening, for the person with whom I had this falling out was my *political philosophy* professor.

I was in her office, we were talking, and the topic of "inequality" arose. Once I suggested that perhaps some of these "inequalities" were due to bad decisions on the part of "the disadvantaged," she quickly responded—and I remember this like it occurred yesterday—that if I insisted upon suggesting that people must assume responsibility for their poverty, that she wouldn't be able to discuss this issue with me further.

Even as I recount this, all of these years later, I am almost as struck now as I was then by the scandalous degree of unprofessionalism and hyper-emotionality that my professor revealed. Her seminar will go down for me as perhaps the single worst course of my years as a college student, for it amounted to little more than an opportunity for her to promote her ideology—an ideology that she shared in common with virtually of all her students.

So why am I bringing all of this up? There are two reasons.

First, my experience at Temple marked a turning point for me. I had always heard of the phenomenon of "indoctrination" to which "conservative" critics of higher education were constantly referring, but I had never actually experienced it. Now I *had* experienced it. Consequently, having become painfully aware of just how severely a professor's abuse of power can stunt a student's intellectual growth, I've learned to empathize with students to an extent that wouldn't have been possible prior to this momentous event.

Second, Jesse Watters, of Fox News, was recently thrown off of the campus of Cornell University. Watters randomly selected Cornell students and asked them whether they were aware that a whopping 96% of the university's faculty political contributions went to *Democrats*.

A recent report in *The Washington Times* reveals what many of us have long known: Cornell, like Temple, isn't at all atypical when it comes to academia.

The *Times* states that, as ranked by U.S. News and World Report, at the nation's 50 top liberal arts colleges, 47 professors have been recorded by the Federal Election Commission as having made political donations to 2016 presidential candidates during the third quarter of this year.

Of those 47 professors, only *one* of them—*only one of them*—gave to a Republican.

The facts render the verdict obvious: Academia is, by and large, a monolith, a bastion of leftist orthodoxy. That there exists far more intellectual homogeneity among academics—i.e. ostensibly intelligent human beings—than is likely to be found anywhere else; and that there exists this degree of homogeneity with respect to topics like politics, morality, and religion, topics over which there is perennial debate, proves that academics don't just *happen* to agree.

Academics *conform*.

This is bad, for in acquiescing in the mentality of the herd, academics betray their vocation, a calling to…*think*. Academics are expected to think *beyond* the clichés and stock phrases of the day, to challenge conventionalities. In not only promoting the PC Zeitgeist, but transforming it into a *creed*, an unassailable body of dogmata, the academic conformist in effect *repudiates* this calling.

So academics harm themselves. Yet they also undermine

the university. The latter is supposed to be a marketplace of ideas, a center of intellectual *diversity*. But insofar as they divest themselves of their own *individuality,* and discourage the cultivation of individuality in their peers, academic conformists preclude diversity.

Academic conformists, however, as well discourage the development of individuality, and, thus, the development of the ability to think, *in students.*

A recent survey—The 2015 Buckley Free Speech Survey—of 800 undergraduate students showed the following:

"By a nearly two-to-one margin, students said their school is generally more tolerant of liberal ideas and beliefs than conservative ideas and beliefs." Only 36% of students polled held that their school was "equally tolerant of both."

Over 60% of students think that "political correctness" is a problem on campus.

Fifty-three percent of students complained that their professors use class time to promulgate *their own* views.

Half of the students surveyed said that "they have often felt intimidated to share beliefs that differ" from their peers, and nearly half remarked that "they have often felt intimidated to share beliefs that differ" from those of their professors.

Seventy percent of students think that their school "should be doing more to promote diversity of opinion."

This survey merely reinforces what has long been common knowledge to many of us.

And it should dispel any questions as to why Jesse Watters was thrown off of Cornell University's campus.

Jack Kerwick

Groupthink in Academia: The Will to Submit

"GROUPTHINK" IS A phenomenon that social psychologists know well. It was in 1972 that Irving Janis first coined the term, and since this time the concept of Groupthink has been applied to the study of decision-making in various contexts.

However, all too rarely have scholars analyzed *academia* in terms of Groupthink. Yet there can be no question that contemporary academics at most universities and colleges throughout America (and beyond) are at least as much as and, truth be told, probably much more so than anyone else under the spell of Groupthink.

I have been teaching philosophy for the last eighteen years. I have taught at a variety of schools from the Southwest to the Northeast, colleges and universities, two-year schools and four-year schools, institutions that are research-oriented and others that are teaching-oriented. I have never ceased to be both intrigued by and incredulous over the political and ideological *conformity* of the vast majority of the members of the academic class.

My intrigue and incredulity stem from the same source: Theoretically, academia is supposed to be a bastion of the free exchange of a rich diversity of ideas. In fact, institutions of *higher* learning are supposed to be *the freest* place for the expression and testing of unconventional, unorthodox theses. According to this ideal, an academic is, almost by definition, a *dissenter*.

The reality, sadly, is an entirely different matter.

While there are always exceptions, faculty in liberal arts and humanities departments are overwhelmingly located squarely on the political left. The latest proof of this—not that any proof is needed for anyone with just the most casual acquaintance with academia—is a study by researchers Mitchell Langbert, Anthony J. Quain, and Daniel B. Klein.

The authors of the study investigated the voter registration of faculty at 40 "leading U.S. universities in the fields of Economics, History, Journalism/Communications, Law, and Psychology." What they found is that of 7,243 professors, 3,623 were registered Democratic while only 314 were registered Republican.

This means that Democrats outnumber Republicans by nearly *twelve to one*.

The ratios of Democrat to Republican for the five disciplines are as follows: Economics (4.5:1); History (33.5:1); Journalism/Communications (20.0:1); Law (8.6:1); and Psychology (17.4:1).

This is remarkable. The researchers admit that while they knew that there are far more Democrats than Republicans in academia, they were surprised to learn that the former outnumbered the latter by this large of a margin.

And many departments at schools throughout America have *zero* Republicans.

Fourteen of the universities canvassed have a Democrat-to-Republican ratio of 20:1 and greater:

Boston College (22:1)
University of North Carolina (23:1)
University of Southern California (26:1)
University of California-Davis (26:1)
University of Maryland (26:1)

Brandeis University (28:1)
Princeton University (30:1)
Columbia University (30:1)
Tufts University (32:1)
Northeastern University (33:1)
Rochester University (35:1)
Johns Hopkins University (35:1)
Boston University (40:1)

These numbers are staggering. Yet none of them come close to *Brown University*, which tops the list with a Democrat:Republican ratio of *60:1*!

Sean Stevens, writing at *Heterodox Academy,* draws a conclusion from the study that is worth noting:

> *While some of this discrepancy [between Democrats and Republicans] may be the result of registered Republicans, and other conservatives, self-selecting out of academia, the sheer size of the discrepancy suggests that self-selection may not be the only factor producing an increasingly left-leaning professoriate.*

Langbert, Quain, and Klein present some hypotheses to account for the overwhelming Democrat-to-Republican ratios in academia. According to most of these, institutional considerations figure prominently. It's not, necessarily, that their hypotheses are wrong; rather, they don't go nearly far enough.

For example, nowhere do the authors note that the ideology shared by most of the inhabitants of the academic world just so happens to be one and the same ideology that pervades all centers of American cultural power and influence: From Washington D.C. to the national news media, from the entertainment industry to the educational industry, the Big

Government-Multi-Cultural-centric creed of leftism or "progressivism" is ubiquitous.

It is like the air that most of us breathe.

This is relevant for at least two reasons.

First, nearly all institutions of higher learning depend upon government-funding for their very existence. With the all-too rare exceptions of those private colleges that are without the partisan imbalances on display virtually everywhere else, colleges and universities today, irrespective of their formal designations as "private" or "public," are overwhelmingly *public* inasmuch as they milk at the breast of the State.

Can it be mere coincidence that academics, in exchange for the dollars that their comrades holding government offices coerce from taxpayers, fuel the very "System" that these self-styled "radicals" pretend to oppose? Can it be mere coincidence that academics, in other words, share and promote the same Politically Correct creed on which the current American Regime relies, a creed that demands the potentially limitless expansion of the State?

Secondly, *fear* is arguably the greatest source of human motivation. The tragic truth is that most people prefer to go-along-to-get-along at *all costs*. Most people, despite imploring their children to resist peer pressure, routinely succumb to the pressure of their own peers. Courage is the rarest of virtues.

Yet it requires tremendous courage to resist the *Zeitgeist*, the "Spirit" of the Times, for it is common knowledge that dissent from PC orthodoxy can come at a psychologically, professionally, and socially ruinous cost. To repeat: The ideology of academia is most definitely *not* limited to academics; it is the ideology of the dominant American (and Western) culture.

As such, in resisting the leftism of their peers, dissident academics can feel like their resisting a force of nature. The alternative—park your brains at the door and join the herd—is clearly the path of least resistance.

This last brings us to a final point. Hannah Arendt was correct in noting a link between moral vice and what she called "the inability to think." It requires *courage* to *think*, to critically assess the reigning orthodoxy. Those who lack courage may have the *ability* to think, but they lack the *willingness* to do so.

This lack of courage, this Will to Submit to the In-Group, I submit, accounts for the Groupthink that prevails among most academics.

Academic Leftism: A Redundancy

RECENTLY, AN ARTICLE featured in *The Chronicle of Higher Education* lamented the lack of "diversity" in my discipline. Philosophy, so goes the article, just hasn't been welcoming toward minorities and women.

Thankfully, such enlightened departments as that found at Penn State University have endeavored to "decolonize the canon."

Of course, academia isn't in the least bit interested in promoting the only diversity that can, or should, mean something in an institution of "higher *learning*." Its equation of "diversity" with gender and racial representation is part of the problem.

Indeed—and I say this as someone who is an academic who happened to have grown up in a lower-middle class neighborhood in Trenton, NJ—there exists far more intellectual diversity at the corner bar than can be found in your average college or university.

Not only does the data confirm the endless anecdotal evidence that legions of academic dissidents like myself have acquired over the years. The data reveals that academics are moving even *further* to *the left*.

The most recent study available was conducted by the University of California. Its findings were released a little more than three years ago in the November of 2012 issue of *Inside Higher Education*.

The study identifies five ideological or political categories: "far left," "liberal," "middle of the road," "conservative," and, finally, "far right." What it finds is that faculty of all ranks from both universities and colleges, institutions that are private and public, large and small, religious and non-religious, self-identified as "far left" to a significantly greater extent than they had just three years earlier: In 2008, 8.8% so self-identified. In 2011, that number had risen to 12.4%.

In glaring contrast, those who self-identified as "far right" *dropped* from—wait for it—0.7% to 0.4%.

However, these numbers alone grossly *understate* the hegemonic rule of leftist thought among faculty on college campuses, for the same study found that the number of self-identified "liberals" *increased* from 47.0% to *50.3%*.

Meanwhile, those in "the middle of the road" *fell* from 28.4% to 25.4%.

As for self-conceived "conservatives," they too *dropped* off from 15.2% to 11.5%.

Even at private Catholic and other Christian colleges and universities, "conservatives" and those on the "far right" constitute a tiny minority. Only 0.3% of the faculty of Catholic institutions locate themselves on the "far right," compared to 7.8% who identify with the "far left," and only 13.3% self-identify as "conservative," compared to *48.0%* who self-identify as "liberal."

At private non-Catholic Christian institutions, "conservatives" have a stronger showing than in any other sector. Yet *even here* they constitute only 23.0% of faculty. On the other hand, "liberals" compose *40.0%* of faculty.

And with 7.4% of the faculty identifying as "far left," the latter has much more of a presence at these private Christian institutions than one would be inclined to think. At any rate, the "far left" has a vastly stronger presence on such campuses than does the "far right," with which only 0.6% of faculty relates.

Writing for *Inside Higher Ed,* Scott Jaschik notes that the leftward trends among faculty have persisted for a long time. George Mason University economics professor, Daniel B. Klein, along with Charlotta Stern, note that in 1972, the ratio of Democrat to Republican in humanities and liberal arts departments was about four-to-one. Today, it is more than eight-to-one. Why?

According to Klein and Stern, academia has the characteristic "antecedent conditions" and "symptoms" of the phenomenon known as "groupthink."

Academics tend to constitute an "insular" and (ideologically) "homogenous" group that, as such, is self-perpetuating, for academics, presiding as they do over decisions pertaining to who will and won't be permitted to join their insiders' club, are disposed to admit those who think like themselves.

Moreover, academics labor under the "illusion of invulnerability" and they share a "belief in the inherent morality of the group" to which they belong. However, "heightened uniformity makes the group overconfident." Consequently, "members take their ideas to greater extremes" but, "facing less testing and challenge," their "habits of thought become more foolhardy and close-minded."

This closed-mindedness is solidified via "collective rationalizations." The authors explain: "Academic professions develop elaborate scholastic dogmas to justify the omission of challenging or intractable ideas." Thus, words like "'normative,' 'ideological,' or 'advocacy'" are used to sweepingly dismiss viewpoints that depart from the mentality of the herd.

Klein and Stern cite Irving Janis, a scholar of groupthink, who remarks that the "reliance on consensual validation" tends to "replace individual critical thinking and reality-testing."

Another sign that academics have succumbed to groupthink is their propensity to indulge in "stereotypes of Out-Groups." Again, Klein and Stern allude to Janis: "One of the symptoms of groupthink is the members' persistence in conveying to each other the cliché and oversimplified images of political enemies embodied in long-standing ideological stereotypes."

Left-leaning academics, as anyone who has spent any amount of time around them can attest, are guilty as sin in this regard: critics are summarily disregarded as "conservatives" or "right-wingers" who, in turn, are associated with the likes of Bill O'Reilly, Rush Limbaugh, George W. Bush, and so forth.

Conservative and classical liberal *thinkers*—like, say, Russell Kirk, F.A. Hayek, Ludwig von Mises, Michael Oakeshott, and Edmund Burke—are rarely, if ever, considered.

"Self-censorship" and "direct pressure on dissenters" are two other "symptoms" of groupthink—and the academic world exemplifies them in spades.

Self-censorship leads to "preference falsification" as academics that disagree with the consensus, rather than express their views, choose instead to go along to get along. Those who dare to step out of line are coerced, in so many ways, to conform. "As the group's beliefs become more defective [questionable], the group becomes more sensitive to tension, more intolerant of would-be challengers and miscreants." Klein and Stern add: "This development leads to tighter vetting and expulsion, more uniformity, more intellectual deterioration, and more intolerance."

It is not toward women and minorities that philosophy and other fields in the humanities are unwelcoming but, rather, those who refuse to endorse leftist groupthink.

Higher Miseducation

Virginia Tech University: Leftist Activism Run Amok, from Top to Bottom

AMONG THE VARIETY of other topics that it explores, my book, *The American Offensive: Dispatches from the Front,* discusses at length the intellectual *and* moral corruption that pervades much of the humanities and liberal arts in the contemporary academy.

The examples of the corruption are legion. Recently, at San Francisco State University, a white student, Cory Goldstein, was accosted, harangued, and assaulted by a black woman—a university employee—for...wearing dreadlocks.

Evidently, Goldstein "micro-aggressed" against this woman specifically and blacks generally, for he is guilty of "cultural appropriation," of appropriating a hair style that is distinctive of "black culture."

"Micro-aggressions," "cultural appropriation"—these are just some of the terms of the esoteric insider-speak to which college students are daily exposed courtesy of their professors.

To repeat, college students are *taught* to view their experiences in terms of the template of *grievance* imposed upon them *by their instructors.*

In a sane world, a world within which people hadn't forgotten that the university is an institution whose *raison d'etre* has been the promotion of Western *civilization,* the ideological abuses to which the academic world has been subjected would constitute nothing less than an epic scandal.

In a sane world, taxpayers wouldn't part with one red cent to subsidize this perversion of the university's historic mission.

But we're not living in a sane world.

Recently, Charles Murray—long-time scholar and co-author of *The Bell Curve,* a study of IQ and its practical implications that was published over 20 years ago—was invited to speak at Virginia Tech University. When, however, certain students got wind of this information, they demanded that the university disinvite him.

Black and white leftist student activists issued a statement in which they charge Murray with being a "social Darwinist" and an agent of "hate" and "prejudice:"

"At the time when rising racism, misogyny and anti-intellectualism have moved to the forefront of our national consciousness," the statement reads, "there is no better place than a college campus from which to focus our efforts against the voices of prejudice and hate [.]"

Murray's "social Darwinist take on intelligence, ability and morality—and his assertion of the inherent inferiority of non-whites and women—do nothing but promote a white supremacist agenda, cast in the guise of 'scientific discourse.'"

Containing as it does all of the vapid, but emotionally-charged and politically effective, buzzwords—"racism," "misogyny," "prejudice," "hate," "social Darwinist," "white supremacist"—this statement, besides being poorly written, is a classic textbook example of precisely the sort of "anti-intellectualism" of which it convicts Murray.

Yet it is no less insubstantial and ideologically-driven than the statement issued by *the faculty* of the Africana Studies Program. The latter accused Murray of being "engaged in a mission to use discredited pseudoscience to perpetuate the subordination of people of African descent, Latino/as, Native

American Indians, the poor, women and the disabled."

Murray's thoughts served to promote a narrative that promised to "visit violence upon marginalized populations—recalling the history of forced sterilization, unjust institutionalization and incarceration, and denial of basic human rights."

Comparison of these two statements, one by students, the other by faculty, is telling in that it underscores what critics of the contemporary university have been saying for far too long: While there is indeed much learning that occurs in our institutions of higher learning, far too little of it is *higher* learning.

Students, that is, are learning from their professors how to become leftist ideologues.

They're learning that "the personal is political" and, as such, both that every aspect of life is politicized *and* that it *must be* politicized in the image of *their* ideology.

Unfortunately, though, they are *not* learning *how to think*.

And if the statement by the faculty of the Africana Studies Program is any indication, students aren't learning how to think because at least some of the faculty isn't up to the task of teaching them.

The faculty statement at Virginia Tech is indistinguishable from that of the students insofar as it consists of such stock terms in vogue as "subordination" and "marginalized populations." Moreover, like that of their student counterparts, faculty too lambast Murray's work as "pseudoscience"—even though, like their students, you can bet dollars to donuts that *none* of them have ever so much as *thought* to read *any* of Murray's scholarship, much less have they read *The Bell Curve*.

In an institution devoted to *education,* instead of political activism, neither faculty nor students would think to regurgitate fallacy-ridden canned statements and uninformed ad hominem attacks against scholars with whom they disagree.

Rather, at an institution of higher learning, both faculty and students would know a thing or two about how to make cogent arguments to substantiate their views, and they would welcome opportunities to genuinely *listen to* and critically engage the exponents of those positions that they question.

But demonizing one's opponents with a little abusive language jammed in between bumper sticker slogans is so much easier than conversing with them. It's easier in that it requires less time, less knowledge, and a whole lot less courage: There's no better way to immunize one's own beliefs against criticism.

As I and others have been contending, the corruption of academia is *systemic*. It isn't just the faculty and student statements at Virginia Tech that reveal this. The administration as well issued a statement that illustrates the groupthink.

Tim Sands, the president of the school, released an "open letter" to the school community. To his credit, he refused to rescind the invitation to Murray. Yet he referred to Murray's work (particularly in *The Bell Curve*) as "largely discredited" and "a flawed socioeconomic theory that has been used by some to justify fascism, racism and eugenics."

"Largely discredited" [read: pseudoscience]; "flawed…theory;" "fascism," "racism," "eugenics": This could've easily been written by any of Virginia Tech's student activists.

Murray replied, claiming that President Sands was "unfamiliar either with the actual content of *The Bell Curve*" or "with the state of knowledge in psychometrics."

My guess is that, like his students and faculty, Sands was unfamiliar *with both*.

Higher Miseducation

Guess what's "Racist" Now? Academic Rigor!

IF YOU'RE A parent who is giving consideration to refinancing your home for the sake of sending your child off to a university, you may want to reconsider.

Most parents, doubtless, regard college as nothing more or less than a means to the end of a lucrative profession for their children. Still, even some of these may be of one mind with those parents who expect that, while pursuing their degrees, their children will and should receive a decent education.

Unfortunately, however, the view of Donna Riley, a professor of engineering education at Purdue University, is representative of a growing number of academics from around the country. In *Rigor/Us: Building Boundaries and Disciplining Diversity with Standards of Merit*, an article featured in the most recent edition of the journal *Engineering Studies,* Riley writes that rigor—"the aspirational quality academics apply to disciplinary standards of quality"—actually "accomplishes dirty deeds" in the fields of "engineering, engineering education, and engineering education research [.]"

To repeat: Academic rigor serves *dirty deeds*.

These "dirty deeds" are "disciplining, demarcating boundaries, and demonstrating white male heterosexual privilege."

Riley trades in the Newspeak that we've come to expect

from contemporary leftist academics. This lends to her prose an aura of Gnosticism, the semblance of esotericism. Ultimately, though, Riley's thesis is hardly original. In fact, it is but another expression of the dogmatic, Politically Correct status quo of her peers. It goes something like this:

Traditional academic standards, being the legacy of straight white men, are not unlike any other legacy of straight white men insofar as they "privilege" straight white men.

In other words, academic standards like that of rigor are "racist," "sexist," "homophobic," "classist," and so forth and so on.

Looking carefully at Riley's "dirty deeds" we see that the act of **disciplining** and the activity of **demarcating boundaries** between academic disciplines or areas of specialization are inseparable from one another. The point seems to be that in carving up the intellectual landscape into distinct domains—in building "walls" or "borders," we might say, between kinds of knowledge—those who are "demarcating" these "boundaries" perpetuate patterns of *exclusion*.

And since it is and has always and only ever been heterosexual white men—or white *males,* as leftists like Riley denigratingly refer to the members of the one group at whose feet they lay the sole blame for all of the things that they think have ever gone wrong in the universe—that have engaged in these activities, "disciplining" and "demarcating boundaries" benefit *them* to the exclusion of all others.

Rigor "is used [by heterosexual white men] to maintain disciplinary boundaries," Riley contends, "with exclusionary implications for marginalized groups and marginalized ways of knowing."

Continuing, she writes that one purpose served by rigor is to function as "a thinly veiled assertion of white male (hetero) sexuality," for the notion of rigor "has a historical lineage of being about hardness, stiffness, and erectness [.]" The "sexual connotations" of rigor, Riley insists, "and [its] links to masculinity in particular…are undeniable."

But Riley goes further. "Rigor may be a defining tool, revealing how structural forces of power and privilege operate to exclude men of color and women, students with disabilities, LGBTQ+ people, first-generation and low-income students, and non-traditionally aged students."

Rigor can be used to "reinforce gender, race, and class hierarchies in engineering, and maintain invisibility of queer, disabled, low-income, and other marginalized engineering students." Ample research, Riley says, substantiates the existence of "a climate of microaggressions and cultures of whiteness and masculinity in engineering."

Riley is blunt, maintaining that "scientific knowledge itself is gendered, raced, and colonizing," and in the field of engineering specifically there is an "inherent masculinist, white, and global North bias" disguised under a mask of "neutrality."

Academic rigor "reproduces inequality," Riley claims. In a nutshell, Riley's argument is powered by the leftist's singular obsession with realizing his *or her* vision of Equality.

However, since this conception of an egalitarian paradise is so wildly at odds with anything that has ever appeared in the real word, leftists like Riley tend to perceive virtually anything and everything as impediments to its realization in the here-and-now. In Riley's case, it leads her to see something as seemingly innocuous, as apparently universal a benefit as academic rigor as an obstacle to she and her fellow ideologues take to be the greatest of moral goods: Equality.

Alternatively stated, and this is important to grasp, because inequality is grossly unjust for the Rileys of the current academic world, such traditional canons of educational excellence as rigor must be viewed as a grave *injustice*.

Rigor, Riley submits, must be "relinquished" entirely, relegated to the dustbin of history (or is it *her*story?). "This is not about reinventing rigor," but, rather, "doing away with the concept altogether so we can welcome other ways of knowing" and "ways of being."

These "other ways" are necessary to help us "critique rigor, and to find a place to start to build a community for *inclusive* and *holistic* engineering education" (emphasis added).

The Racism-Industrial-Complex (RIC) is a sprawling industry with tentacles reaching into practically every area of our culture. There is no place that it has impacted to quite the degree that it has impacted academia. In fact, the emergence and growth of RIC has corresponded to and fueled the emergence and growth of the *Academic-Industrial-Complex*. The two intersect and blend with one another.

Parents with college-bound children, particularly (but certainly not only) *white* parents, should bear this in mind.

College "Common Reading" Programs are as "Progressive" as you Think

DEPENDING ON THE institution of one's choice, those who are planning to enter college for the first time in the fall may be expected to read an assigned book over the summer. That is, many schools have a "common reading program," a program designed to insure that incoming students read the same book before embarking upon their college career.

As the National Association of Scholars has amply demonstrated in its recent *Beach Books Report* (BBR), the ideological indoctrination of college students can't begin quickly enough.

The BBR is a study of 348 institutions of higher learning. This includes 171 public four-year schools, 81 private sectarian schools, 70 private nonsectarian institutions, and 26 community colleges. Fifty-eight of these schools were identified by *U.S. News & World Report* as among the top 100 universities in the country, while 25 are among the top 100 liberal arts colleges. The colleges and universities covered by the BBR report are located in 46 states and Washington D.C.

What the study found is that colleges "rarely assign" classic texts, making "the common reading genre...parochial, contemporary, and progressive." In fact, 75% (271) of the common reading books were published between 2010 and 2016 while 94% (327) were published between 2000 and 2016.

The books were all published during the lifetime of the students.

As for the most popular subjects and themes, anyone who knows anything at all about contemporary academia won't be surprised by the BBR's findings.

For the academic year 2016-2017, the study's authors ascribed to the common readings 576 subject labels that are divided into 30 subject categories. "The most popular subject categories," it states, "were Civil Rights/Racism/Slavery (74 readings), Crime and Punishment (67 readings), Media/Silence/Technology (34 readings), Immigration (32 readings), and Family Dysfunction/Separation (31 readings)."

The BBC also broke the readings down into 251 theme labels and 18 theme categories. That most of these "register the common reading committees' persisting interest in 'diversity,' defined by non-white ethnicity at home and abroad," is hardly unexpected to readers of this column. Some other findings, though, while anything but shocking, are nevertheless telling.

"Many common readings discuss books of which a film or television version exists, an increasing number are graphic novels [what used to be called "comic books"] or memoirs, many have a protagonist under 18 or simply young-adult novels, and a significant number have an association with National Public Radio (NPR)."

Comic books; young-adult novels; books based on popular films and TV shows and associated with *NPR*—this is much of the stuff of common reading programs.

The BBR summarizes its findings:

> *The themes register most strongly the common reading genre's continuing obsession with race, as well as the infantilization of its students, its middlebrow taste, and*

its progressive politics.

Indeed. This past academic year, "the most popular themes were African-American (103), Latin American (25), Protagonist Under 18 (25), African (15), and Islamic World (13)."

For the last three consecutive years, "Racism/Civil Rights/Slavery and Crime and Punishment were the two most popular subject categories," and "African-American themes were…the most popular theme [.]" These subjects and themes became even more popular this past year than they had been in the two preceding years.

The "top books" for common reading illustrate this trend. The most routinely assigned text is Bryan Stevenson's, *Just Mercy: A Story of Justice and Redemption.* This is a work of nonfiction. The theme is "African-American" and the subject categories are "Civil Rights/Racism/Slavery" and "Crime and Punishment."

Then there is Ta-Nehisi Coates' memoir, *Between the World and Me.* The theme is "African-American," and the subject categories are "Civil Rights/Racism/Slavery" and "Crime and Punishment."

Wes Moore's memoir, *The Other Wes Moore: One Name, Two Fates,* is another hit. Its theme is "African-American" and its subject categories are "Crime and Punishment" and "Poverty."

Malala Yousafzai's memoir, as written by Christina Lamb, is quite popular. *I Am Malala: The Girl Who Stood Up for Education and Was Shot by the Taliban* has an "Islamic World theme." Its subject categories are "Education" and "Feminism/Sex Discrimination/Women."

Of the six remaining most popular books in the common reading genre, the themes are: "African-American," "Muslim-American," "Asian American," "Latin American," and "Protagonist under 18." One book, a fictional novel, doesn't have a specifically designated theme.

The BBR laments that the "ideologically-constrained common reading genre has become so homogenous that common reading selections have become predictable." These reading programs are designed to advance a "progressive message" or "dogma through discussion guides, question prompts, and cooperation with 'social justice' programs." They are also meant to "promote activism," thus neglecting "the virtues of the disengaged life of the mind."

This preference for inculcating activism over the love of knowledge for its own sake, ideology over education, has resulted in an intellectual flaccidity that has become an all too salient feature on college campuses. "Common reading programs make new students' first experience in college 'co-curricular,' and so tell students that the heart of college is not the regular academic coursework but the 'co-curriculum.'" Their mission statements "usually direct committees to fulfill non-academic goals, such as *building community* or *inclusivity*" (emphases original).

For parents who plan upon remortgaging their homes so as to subsidize their children's four year (or more) excursion to the university, the National Association of Scholars' "Beach Books Report" is must reading.

Mizzou: A Textbook Case of the Triumph of Barbarity over Civility in Higher Ed

DUE TO DEMANDS by student activists and their enablers on the staff and faculty of University of Missouri, the President and Chancellor have now resigned.

Good riddance.

Neither Tom Wolfe nor R. Bowen Loftin deserves an iota of sympathy. In fact, they are at least as contemptible as the lynch mob that drove them from their offices, for they had been every bit as guilty as the professors and football coaches who have spent years pandering to the sophomoric bullies who society expected for them to *educate*.

This last point bears repeating: The University of Missouri, like the overwhelming majority of America's institutions of "higher learning," exists on the taxpayer's dime. No college, no student, is entitled to one penny that belongs to someone else. That society subsidizes Mizzou implies a duty—*a duty!*—on the part of the latter to make its students into educated, self-disciplined, law-abiding citizens.

Wolfe, Loftin, and Mizzou's football coaches and faculty have failed miserably on this score. They have reneged on their contract with the rest of us. They have *betrayed* their American compatriots, including those millions and millions of working-class and middle-class Americans who labor diligently day after day and week after week only to have a portion of their earnings confiscated and redistributed to grease the wheels of the Academic-Industrial-Complex.

Mizzou's football players refused to play anymore games until Wolfe had resigned. Had he been committed to discharging his obligation to the taxpayer, to say nothing of his obligation to the school community, he would have deprived the football players of their scholarships, expelled them from school, and terminated the coaches who backed them.

Of course, the University of Missouri is but a microcosm of the contemporary scene in academia: the worst of vices—cowardice, hypocrisy, obsequiousness, hyper-emotionality, rigorous anti-intellectualism, self-aggrandizement, and many others—exemplified by the administrators, faculty, staff, and students at Mizzou are legion throughout the academic world.

Higher education is Big Education. The causes for the intellectual and moral rot of the university are admittedly various. Yet one huge cause is the university itself.

If students *really* are under the delusion that "racism," "sexism," and the like are omnipresent in, of all places, such bastions of left-wing "progressive" ideology as the college campus, it is because their professors and school administrators have worked tirelessly, obsessively even, to convince them that this is so.

So too has the young's wildly exaggerated sense of self-importance been fueled in no small measure by the same suspects.

The product of the poisonous combination of these two flights of fancy—victimhood and narcissism—is *barbarism.*

Barbarians don't *discuss*; they *demand*. Barbarians don't *remonstrate;* they *coerce*. Barbarians don't' have *interlocutors*. In fact, they don't even see *opponents*.

Barbarians see *enemies*.

And because they are *enemies* who, as such, are outside of the orbit of the tribe, a barbarian's enemies must, in effect, be reduced to the status of, not just non-*persons*, but non-*entities*.

This explains why the student and faculty barbarians at Mizzou demanded not just the resignation of Tom Wolfe, but his complete social annihilation: Among their list of demands was the demand that Wolfe write a *hand-written letter* in which he confesses to his "negligence"—i.e. his racial insensitivity or, what amounts to the same thing, his "racism." Then, he was ordered to hold a *press conference* in *the student center* where he would read from his letter aloud.

To reiterate, the barbarians of Mizzou didn't demand that Wolfe do all of this *in lieu of* resigning. They demanded that he grovel and disgrace himself *in addition to* leaving his post.

In other words, the barbarians didn't just want victory over Wolfe. As is their way, they sought to *humiliate* and *degrade* him.

Wolfe and Loftin didn't meet all of these demands—even if they did in fact do some groveling before they eventually resigned. The point, though, is that their failure is now complete, for, courtesy of their spinelessness, student barbarians everywhere—as well as *everyone* else—now know that barbarianism is a winning ticket.

The University of Missouri is a classic textbook case of how and why barbarity trumps civility on today's college campus.

Jack Kerwick

College Campus Hostility

I HEAR THAT there is a new book that just hit the presses: *No Campus for White Men: The Transformation of Higher Education into Hateful Indoctrination,* by Scott Greer, a young white man himself who graduated from college only about five years ago. I plan on reading his work soon.

That being said, that there is a campaign of sorts on far too many college campuses against whites, males, and, especially, white men, as Greer says, is practically self-evident to anyone who has paid attention to academia for any length of time. Parents, particularly the parents of whites and white males, should pay especially close attention to this tragic phenomenon.

Due to space constraints, I implore parents with college-bound children to mull over the following two examples—illustrations, mind you, that it took me all but a minute to find. They are indeed, unfortunately, representative of the contemporary academic scene.

> (1) At elite Brown University we find "Brown Survivors Speak" (BSS), a student organization that ostensibly exists for the sake of providing support to female students who are rape victims. Yet the group's standard operating procedure has been to "out" and "shame" those who have been *accused* of rape. It encourages women who allege to have been raped to

write the names of their attackers in the Women's restroom stalls in Brown's library.

BSS also publishes the name of the accused in a Google form that it posts on its Facebook page.

Recently, the group was forced to reconsider its methods as it conceded that it "outed," not a rapist, but an *innocent* person. Moreover, others, purporting to be innocent, complained that they never even knew that their names had been included on BSS's list of aggressors. One student whose name wound up on the list was incredulous when this was revealed to him. He complained that it marked students with a "moral stain" that, he feared, would remain with them even after charges had been found to be "unsubstantiated."

Defacing school property and branding potentially innocent people as rapists—this is what is permitted to transpire at one of the most elite academic institutions in the country.

(2) Matters are at least as troublesome at small private colleges too. Take St. Olaf College, a Lutheran institution in rural Minnesota.

This past weekend, a young black female student claims to have found a typed-written note that someone had left for her on the windshield of her car. It reads: "I am so glad that you are leaving soon. One less n****r to deal with. You have spoken up too much. You will change nothing. Shut up or I will shut you up." The young woman posted a picture of the note on social media and, consequently, aggrieved students (apparently, not all of whom were black) took over campus.

The College Fix interviewed Katherine Hinderaker, of the

College Republicans at St. Olaf. "The students have taken over the campus like a coup," she remarked. Among the buildings that the mob surrounded is the school cafeteria. Hinderaker continued, explaining that when her friend tried sneaking into the dining area from the rear, the hostiles ran and blocked the entrance.

One student, she heard, was assaulted.

Describing what she took to be the mentality of the mob, Hinderaker stated: "The idea is, 'we feel uncomfortable every day so we are going to make you feel uncomfortable."

Hinderaker left campus on Saturday night so that she could bring food and fluids back to those students who routinely rely upon the school cafeteria—the cafeteria that their peers prevented them from using as they railed against "institutional racism."

The mob stormed the library as well. A female student employee was reportedly pushed when she refused to yield to its demand that she turn over an intercom mic. The mobsters—"the demonstrators"—forced not just the mic from her. When she tried to call campus security, they tore the phone out of the wall.

The disruptors set up signs in the commons area that they occupied. The signs read: "I'm sick of white tears" and "F**k your white complacency."

One anonymous student informed The College Fix: "The campus admins are allowing the commons area to become a bulletin board of complaints against white people. No action has been taken to remove the signs, and no students dare to touch them since there are newly-installed cameras everywhere."

Faculty cancelled their classes this past Monday so that students who originally wanted to boycott the school and hold it accountable for the "institutionalized racism that is embedded within the structures of the campus" could do so. The students drew up an "extensive" list of demands, as the aggrieved themselves describe it.

An administrator, an assistant to "the president for institutional diversity," made a statement. The college, he said, cancelled all classes on Monday (May 1) "so that we may have time for faculty, students, and staff to continue the discussions about racism and diversity on our campus."

Neither this administrator nor the head honcho, President David Anderson, uttered a word of criticism of the thuggery in which minority students had engaged. Instead, Anderson condemned the note that the black female student claimed had been left for her as "a despicable and cowardly act" that "violates all of our values as a college and a community."

The mob, however, was not impressed by his obsequiousness. A video is available that features students treating him with all of the courtesy that college leftists can be expected to reserve for conservative speakers. Even as Anderson was busy assuring them that the school is deploying all of its available resources to determine the identity of those responsible for the note, the student agitators were just as busy interrupting and yelling at him.

And, to repeat, no official at St. Olaf condemned, much less punished, the coercive and intimidating tactics of the "protesters." No one condemned, much less punished, the racial animus that they overtly expressed toward their white peers.

Parents and, when appropriate, taxpayers, must unequivocally condemn and punish administrators who continue to allow faculty and student activists to promote racial and other bigotries within the college communities over which they preside.

Jack Kerwick

Christophobia on College Campus: A Muslim Teacher vs. A Christian Student

EACH NEW DAY brings new stories from around the country of life on college campuses. It seems that an increasing number of these stories are cause for lamentation.

Consider the recent case at Rollins College, a private, four-year institution in Florida. Marshall Polston, a 20 year-old sophomore, is a self-described Christian and an honors student. Not long ago, he had been suspended from school upon having had a few unpleasant experiences with the Islamic professor of his Middle Eastern Humanities class.

Polston told *The College Fix* that his professor, Areej Zufari, insisted in class that Jesus's disciples did not believe that He was divine. She also reportedly said that He was never actually crucified.

In other words, Zufari allegedly expressed the standard Islamic viewpoint on Jesus.

Polston's problem with his instructor, however, was not primarily with her position. It's that she asserted it as "academic fact" when it is anything but that.

And he let Zufari know as much during class.

Shortly afterwards, though, the student received a shock when he received a 52% on one of his assignments. Suspecting that his uncharacteristically low grade was retribution for the challenges that he posed to Zufari's depiction of Christianity, Polston fired off a lengthy email to her—an email that she turned over to administrators and that resulted in his suspension.

This penalty was felt all that much more acutely when Polston considered that, during class discussion, an Islamic student faced not so much as a verbal warning when he remarked that under Sharia law adulterers and gays deserved decapitation. Polston told *The Fix* that "the conservative Muslim student" aroused "such fear by some" of the students by his remark that one of them contacted the FBI about it.

But it was *Polston* who Professor Zufari reported to the Dean of Campus Safety.

Zufari didn't let the matter rest at that, however. Via Facebook, she posted to the ACLU her complaint regarding Polston—even though she didn't identify him by name. Zufari described him as someone who was "making my life hell this semester." Polston, she said, "is spewing hatred at me, de-railing class, and just sent me a hateful email threatening me."

Zufari concluded by inquiring as to whether "there is a way to hold the individual responsible for his harassment and hate speech."

Hate speech? If a Christian student is guilty of "spewing hatred" for taking issue with an instructor for presenting as false events that his faith affirms and that, at any rate, many historians accept as true (the crucifixion of Jesus and the belief on the part of His disciples that He was divine), then academia has become an unwelcoming place indeed for Christian students. More accurately, it has become a bastion of hostility to anyone who would dare to challenge historically dubious assertions.

Yet maybe it was the content of Polston's email to Zufari that the latter found "hateful" and "harassing." It's clear that Polston did not mince words. He accused Zufari of being "extremely unfair" and pursuing "a ruthless program of hostility" in her grading of his work all because he objected to her "inherent bias and clandestine theological apologies."

Polston, who reminded Zufari that he spoke with her personally before his paper was due to make sure that he understood all of the directions, accused Zufari of assigning him an undeserved grade in order to "silence" him in class.

It's true that Polston did accuse Zufari of "incompetence," of being "a failure as a Professor," of "brainwashing" students about the Politically Incorrect realities of Sharia law in the Middle East, of "indoctrinating." Zufari, Polston continued, belongs in "reform school," not in an institution of higher learning.

He also said that she acted in a "cowardly" and "sick" manner inasmuch as she viewed "my intellectual conversation" as "more threatening than the despicable comments about decapitation" made by a Muslim student. Polston as well "threatened" Zufari—but he threatened to go to her dean and, if need be, the media.

He did *not* threaten her physically.

While Polston certainly made it clear that he was angry with his instructor, and while some of his comments doubtless could only be taken as insults by Zufari, it's difficult to see how anything that he had said or did rises to the level of *harassment,* much less *hatred.*

Evidently, the same administration that suspended him came to agree with this verdict, for Polston was reinstated after a week of being suspension.

While cleared of the more serious charges that were filed against him—Zufari alleged that Polston made her feel "unsafe"—he was still reprimanded for being "aggressive, disrespectful, and at times vulgar in multiple verbal and electronic communications with faculty, staff and students."

Though his instructor's more serious allegations against

him had been found baseless, and while he feels vindicated, Polston is still considering filing a lawsuit against Zufari. His lawyer, Kenneth Lewis, stated in a press release that, upon having leveled indefensible allegations against his client, Rollins College must consider whether Zufari has "fitness to continue…in any capacity" at the school. Lewis maintains that the instructor tried to "destroy" Polston's academic future "for merely questioning her academic validity."

There may be more to this story, but one thing is for certain: Given the rise in educational malpractice, the rise of intolerance of those viewpoints that deviate from the leftist orthodoxy that prevails on America's college campuses, Polston's account of his ordeal is all too plausible.

If professors refrained from pushing the party line in class; if they instead taught their students how, not what, to think; then perhaps we would never hear of the Marshall Polstons of the world.

Jack Kerwick

Higher Ed: No "Safe Spaces" for Students who Refuse

IT WOULD APPEAR that higher education has become a Politically Correct caricature of itself. Yet for an increasing number of students, this is no laughing matter, for academia's ceaseless drift toward the abyss of far-left ideology has been accompanied by an increase in threats of violence.

College campuses in many places have become *dangerous* for certain kinds of students.

Specifically, they have become dangerous for *conservative* students.

The College Fix (*TCF*) is a student-run publication. It is also a national treasure. Its writers deserve praise for drawing the public's attention to the outrages that pass for higher education today. Parents should be particularly appreciative to learn that those of their children who they plan on sending to university could be harassed and threatened with violence for not endorsing the ideological groupthink that substitutes for education in the contemporary academic world.

At St. Olaf College, a Lutheran institution in Minnesota, Republican and conservative-leaning students are overwhelmingly outnumbered. In November, 80% of its student body voted for Hillary Clinton. Only 10% voted for President Donald Trump.

Yet there are no "safe spaces" for this minority.

TCF quotes the school's student newspaper, the *Manitou Messenger*. The latter interviewed 12 Trump supporting students, virtually "all" of whom admitted to feeling that the campus environment rendered it impossible for them to discuss—civilly, rationally discuss—politics with their peers. But it is even worse than this, given that "several" of these students had been "violently threatened because of their political beliefs [.]"

On the night of the election, the President of the College Republicans, Emily Schaller, was threatened by another student and called a "f**king moron." In the days following Trump's victory, she overheard groups of students promising aloud "to hurt the next conservative or Republican they saw."

The Vice President of the College Republicans, another young lady, Kathryn Hinderaker, encountered the same phenomenon.

She told her school paper that "one of the hardest things" occurred the day after the presidential election. It was at that time that, upon entering a campus building, she heard someone shout assurances to all Trump voters that they had "better be f**king scared!" To this, all who were present "clapped and applauded."

"Obviously," she concludes, "it didn't feel super safe."

It doesn't take an especially creative intellect to imagine what the reaction of the whole college community would have been had it not been Republican and Trump-supporting students, but, say, immigrant or black students that had been threatened in this manner. Nor does it require much prescience to know that had the female students that were victimized been leftist feminists, the reaction to their victimization would have been far different from what it has been.

One student—another female—remarked that such was the hostility of the environment in her classes toward "conservatives" that she left school for a time. By the end of the fall semester, the on-line harassment that she endured drove her to transfer to another institution altogether.

In February, someone "posted an unsolicited photo of a group of students that supposedly included Trump supporters and encouraged fellow students to 'remember their faces.'"

Ironically, St. Olaf College's chapter of the College Republicans did *not* endorse Trump during the election season. However, its members are still targeted. Conservative students will not express their views in class for fear of being ostracized or injured by their peers and penalized by their instructors.

For some students, the toxicity of the campus environment has gotten to be too much. For about 20 minutes at the beginning of every class period, said one female pupil, her professor would mock Trump. This student said that she planned on transferring to another institution next year.

While some of their students were being mocked, intimidated, and threatened for their viewpoints, the administrators and faculty of St. Olaf College extended their collective arms in welcoming the one-time Communist Party USA presidential candidate Angela Davis to speak on campus.

Time doesn't permit it, but, tragically, it wouldn't require much effort to show that St. Olaf College is not anomalous in these respects. Conservative students are threatened, bullied, intimidated, and, on occasion, assaulted at colleges and universities around the country. Worse, it is not always just their fellow students who target them, but professors as well.

In the meantime, and for all of their hysteria concerning the need for "cry ins," safe spaces, and the like, radical leftist students and faculty speak and act with impunity.

Other examples of this educational malpractice, intolerance, and outright oppression will be revisited in this column in the near future. Everyone who cares about protecting the victims of injustice while salvaging what can be salvaged of higher education in America needs to both inform themselves of this crisis and work diligently to resolve it.

Evergreen State College: The Chickens Are Coming Home to Roost

WHEN I WAS a teenager, I spent much of my time getting involved in all sorts of things that I should have avoided, and knew then that I should have avoided.

One of these activities was fist fighting.

It's been many years since I was a teenager, and nearly as many years since I've been in a physical confrontation with anyone. At 21, I renewed the baptismal promises of my childhood faith of (Roman Catholic) Christianity and redirected my life, turning from my own little selfish world to that of politics and education.

What I never could have imagined all of those years ago, and what I still couldn't have imagined until quite recently, is that American politics generally and Higher Education specifically would become fertile ground for the very violence from which, I was delusional enough to once think, they would provide relief.

The student-thuggery that cowardly administrators and faculty have permitted, indeed, have encouraged, at colleges and universities around the country is one such topic that makes this academic's blood boil.

Take Evergreen State College as exhibit one. I have written

Jack Kerwick

about Evergreen recently, so I won't bother to rehash all of the ugly details that I recounted here. The gist of the situation is this: A leftist professor, Bret Weinstein, registered his opposition to the new format of his school's annual "Day of Absence." Each year, black students, faculty, and staff would stay home so that their white counterparts could attend racial sensitivity workshops and the like while acquiring an appreciation for the plethora of ways in which nonwhites enrich Evergreen—or something like this.

This year, though, the racial roles were reversed and whites were essentially told that *they must* stay home. Weinstein, who had no objections to the annual tradition, objected to the fact that, unlike in the past, whites were being *coerced*, on the basis of skin color, to avoid the college.

In response, black students accosted, harassed, and physically threatened Weinstein and those of his students who supported him. On social media, they threatened to "dox" the latter. Weinstein had to be escorted and, soon afterwards, barred from campus, for the police expressly told him that they could not guarantee his safety.

Let this register: A professor who did nothing other than object to a race-based, coercive policy can't return to *a college campus* for fear of being injured *by students*.

What's worse is that his pusillanimous colleagues and supervisors in the administration have sided with the thugs. At his "meeting" with them, these punk bullies shouted and cursed at the President of Evergreen State, George Bridges. They mocked and insulted him, calling Bridges by his first name: "F**k YOU GEORGE, we don't wanna listen to a GODDAMN thing you have to say! No, you shut the f**k up!"

Perhaps most appalling of all, these "protesters" expressed what can only be described as the worst sort of Black supremacy as they recycled racist clichés that one would swear they took from the Nation of Islam's book of fictions. This one is a gem:

"We been here before you," one of the students remarked to Bridges. "We [blacks] built these cities, we [blacks] had civilization way before you [whites] ever had…comin' out your caves."

Of course, the black supremacist agitators peppered their eloquent oratory with such profound turns of phrase as: "Whiteness is the most violent f**kin' system to ever breathe!" and "These white-ass faculty members need to be holding HIM [President Bridges], and HIM, and ALL these people accountable!"

They chanted "black power" and "F**K YOU, and F**K THE POLICE!"

In spite of the abuse to which his tormentors subjected him—or maybe *because* of it?—Bridges *thanked* the mob and promised to meet their demands. One of Weinstein's colleagues, a woman who, according to what he told podcast host Joe Rogan, is not white, accused him of provoking a "white supremacist backlash" against the student mob.

So far, these black supremacists haven't come close to facing any disciplinary action. Quite the contrary, the very administration that they have bullied, threatened, and intimidated has bent over backwards to reinforce their arrogance.

This whole spectacle should outrage decent people of all races. Evergreen accepts federal monies. Americans should demand that not a penny of their income be spent subsidizing this rot. We should demand that these students be expelled and charged with racial "hate crimes." The administrators who have allowed this rot to fester should be summarily terminated and those faculty, like, sad to say, Professor Weinstein himself, who invested years into cultivating the leftist ideology of Political Correctness (which includes the dogma of Racial Correctness), should be compelled to sit through an indefinite number of hours of diversity training, yes, but *intellectual* diversity training.

Granted, this last prescription may not be feasible. I offer it tongue-in-cheek—sort of. The point, though, is that for as much as Weinstein deserves to be commended for his courage, the fact of the matter remains that the corruption of consciousness that plagues Evergreen's blacktivist students, the wickedness that they're unleashing upon the whole school community, is a function of the wickedness of the ideology that they've imbibed courtesy of the Weinsteins of academia.

The students' gross incivility, arrogance, and ignorance, comprehensively, their lapse into barbarism, reflects the quality of the education, or lack of education, at Evergreen. These vices are the poisonous fruits of the leftist creed of their faculty and administrators.

Weinstein deserves our support, but he also needs to know that the students who now threaten him and his students are the monster to the Dr. Frankenstein of his own ideology.

More Groupthink in Academia

ACCORDING TO THE campus watchdog organization *The College Fix,* run by students, the political donations of Duke University employees are *ten times* higher in the year since Donald Trump was elected to the presidency than they were in the year following the reelection of Barack Obama.

The Center for Responsive Politics found that Duke faculty and staff members made 870 individual contributions within the last year. This number is in stark contrast with the 88 individual contributions that they made over the span of 2013.

What's telling, but unsurprising, is that of the 870 political contributions made by Duke University employees, all but *six* were made to leftist, Democratic Party causes and candidates.

Sadly, the ideological and political homogeneity that prevails at Duke is all too representative of that which imbues the contemporary academic world:

In the social sciences, Democrats outnumber Republicans nearly *twelve-to-one*. This is the finding of research into five fields—economics, journalism, history, psychology, and law—at 40 "leading" universities.

The researchers admitted that the Democrat-to-Republican ratio is "even higher" than they had suspected, and that it is highest at the more prestigious universities. They also found that "an awful lot of departments have zero Republicans."

At Columbia University, in the five disciplines on which

the study focuses, there were a total of 179 registered Democrats and a total of *six* registered Republicans. This is a Democrat: Republican ratio of nearly *30 to one*. Yet of the 40 universities studied, Columbia still came in at having only the *ninth* highest Democrat-to-Republican ratio behind eight other institutions.

Caltech and Worchester Polytechnic Institute, which came in at first (13:0) and second places (9:0), respectively, are technical institutions with significantly lower overall numbers than are typical of the generic university. Yet they rank as high as they do because they have *zero* Republicans in the fields in question. In third, fourth, fifth, sixth, seventh, and eighth places are Brown University (60:1); Boston University (40:1); John Hopkins (35:1); Rochester University (35:1); Northeastern University (33:1); and Tufts University (32:1).

In total, this study "looked up 7,243 professors and found 3,623 to be registered Democratic and 314 [registered] Republican." The remaining weren't registered with either party.

It has long been common knowledge among those in the know that while institutions of higher education should be the most intellectually free and diverse places in the world, in reality they are anything but this. Quite the contrary: a remotely objective, casual observer of academia can't fail to be struck by the ideological and political uniformity pervading American faculty.

Indeed, Groupthink is as visible in academia as it is anywhere. Actually, it is more prevalent in academia than it is almost anywhere.

The social psychologist Irving Janis characterized the phenomenon that he referred to as "Groupthink" in terms of the following symptoms:

(1) The illusion of invulnerability

(2) Collective rationalization
(3) Belief in inherent morality
(4) Stereotyped views of out-groups
(5) Direct pressure on dissenters
(6) Self-censorship
(7) Illusion of unanimity
(8) Self-appointed "mindguards"

When it is considered that *the* in-group of academia is powered by a "progressivist" vision, Janis's "symptoms" seem that much more fitting:

(1) The illusion of invulnerability, as Janis labeled it, generates "excessive optimism that encourages taking extreme risks." Historically, and much to the chagrin of its countless victims, excessive optimism and the extreme risk-taking to which it leads are hallmarks of leftist ideology in action.

(2) As for collective rationalization, this transpires inasmuch as the group's members fail to revisit their presuppositions—even after others warn them as to the disastrous consequences to which their plans could lead. Again, one will not be hard pressed to find illustrations of leftists ignoring warnings and clinging to the assumptions underwriting the destructive policies that they continue to support.

(3) Members' belief in the inherent morality of the group's causes is actually a belief in the moral *superiority* of those causes and, thus, the concomitant conviction that the pursuit and realization of those causes are without any

objectionable consequences.

(4) The in-group needs an "enemy," an out-group that it can demonize. We see how the left, whether in academia or elsewhere, satisfies this need today. Members of out-groups are "stereotyped" as "racists," "sexists," "homophobes," "Islamophobes," "white supremacists," "colonialists," "capitalists," "the rich," etc.

(5) Members of the in-group, or at least those who are believed to be members, are pressured to resist deviating in any key respects from the party line. Examples of this "symptom" of Groupthink in academia abound, with dissenting left-liberal academics being treated at least as scornfully as those to their right who belong to the out-group: Blacks who are deemed by the members of the in-group of being insufficiently progressive are derided as "sell-outs," "oreos," "race-traitors," and worse, while women who incur the academic left's wrath find that their womanhood is denied to them.

And, of course, if the deviant is a white liberal man, then he is ultimately objectified as a "racist" and "white supremacist."

The bottom line is that dissent, at least over certain fundamental propositions, is not tolerated by the in-group.

(6) That this last message is usually received loudly and clearly is borne out by the fact that the members of the in-group censor themselves: Seeing the fate of those of their fellow members

who have dared to challenge the orthodoxy of the group, individual members of the academic clique will suppress their thoughts when they are at odds with the group's orthodoxy.

(7) The illusion of unanimity is strong among academic leftists. It is indeed assumed that the majority perspective is the perspective of all of their colleagues.

(8) "Mindguards" are those members of the group—this would be whole departments at most colleges and universities around the country—that strive to immunize the ideology of the group against any potential threats to it.

There is much more that needs to be said on this subject of academic Groupthink. Far too few studies have as yet to be done on it.

However, as I was at pains to show here, there can be no question that Groupthink does in fact exist among contemporary academics.

Jack Kerwick

Threats to Conservative Students: What are Faculty and Administrators Doing About It?

WHETHER IT IS female Republican students at places like St. Olaf College and Cornell University being accosted, cursed at, threatened with physical violence and, in the latter case, actually assaulted; Cal State Fullerton Trump supporting students being assaulted by an *instructor;* a riot at Berkeley; or College Republicans being targeted by name as "fascists" and encouragements made to make their personal information public so that decent folks can "punch fascists"—bullying, intimidation, and threats of violence against conservative students have become a staples of campus life.

While this phenomenon is an outrage in itself, equally outrageous is the fact that it has been permitted to occur and recur.

Now, imagine that in each of the foregoing cases it was self-avowed feminist, black, Hispanic, gay, Muslim, and transgender students that had to endure this hostility courtesy of Republican, conservative, and Trump-supporting peers. "Social Justice" activists would see to it that it was national news and administrators would be bending over backwards to show the world that they were cracking down on the "bigotry."

Since, in reality, it is only conservative and moderate

students who are being victimized by leftists, administrators and faculty have done little to nothing to stop the abuses that their non-leftist students have suffered. And, in some instances, they have even encouraged the attacks.

In October of last year, the Young Conservatives of Texas (YCT) held a bake sale at the University of Texas that was designed to expose the moral dubiousness of "affirmative action." Goods were sold to blacks and Hispanics for prices that were lower than those that whites and Asians were expected to pay.

Consequently, leftist students surrounded their display and shouted at them to remove it. One such student livestreamed the event on Facebook in a post titled, "Racists are live at UT." It received nearly 230,000 views.

Eventually, students sporting black masks stole the bake sale menu and raided the inventory.

The Vice President for Diversity and Community Engagement, Dr. Gregory J. Vincent, was the only administrator from UT to issue a formal response to the incident.

Vincent blamed the conservative students.

Their bake sale, he claimed, "create[d] an environment of exclusion and disrespect among our students, faculty, and staff," and their methods are "counterproductive to true dialogue on our campus" and "unrepresentative of the ideals toward which our [UT] community strives."

Vincent didn't deny that the Young Conservatives of Texas were exercising their right to express themselves. However, he declared that in doing so, they "resorted to exercising one of the university's core values to the detriment of others."

At College of Charleston campus, in South Carolina, not only does faculty provide no support to conservative students who, at least since the election, have felt increasingly uneasy on campus and in their classes. Faculty is largely responsible for the apprehensiveness.

Rachel McKinnon is an instructor of philosophy and a self-identified "queer woman." Immediately after the election, she used her class time to hold a "cry in" of sorts where she offered her grieving students comfort candy. McKinnon too was "shaken" by Trump's victory. At one point she pounded her lectern and, in response to a student who tried assuring her that the South Carolina legislature would not permit the new administration to strip gays and the transgendered of their rights, condescendingly "snapped": "Where do you think we are?"

Students and, in some cases, their parents, have been leveling complaints. One mother called the President's office and suggested that McKinnon had a "mental breakdown" and was "silencing conservative students in class."

McKinnon's colleague Jon Hale, a history professor, organized a faculty meeting with the school's provost, Brian McGee, to discuss the oppressive environment that was developing for…*faculty*.

According to a South Carolina newspaper, the Post and Courier, those present at the meeting sought to "challenge" McGee on his administration's position on "academic freedom."

The Provost had sent an email to the deans and chairs of the school's departments about complaints that his office had been receiving regarding the "inappropriately one-sided" and "crudely partisan" nature of class discussions.

Another email sent to the whole college community insisted that "no matter the political divide, we must always be tolerant of each other's views."

A few weeks later, McGee announced the creation of a new on-line complaint system for students.

From the perspective of those who want for conservative students to be treated fairly, all of this sounds encouraging, and Provost McGee sounds like he deserves a tip of the hat.

However, McGee assured concerned faculty that the complaint system was being implemented only because it was required by the school's regional accrediting agency. It was "spectacularly bad timing" on his part, McGee confessed, to have announced the creation of this system when he did, for the timing of the announcement wrongly led faculty to think that the system was a response to complaints about their politicization of their class discussions.

Moreover, McGee assured faculty that his administration would protect them from any efforts on the part of the state Legislature to interfere with the manner in which they ran their classes.

The bullying, intimidation, and threats with which conservative students are confronted at present largely go unmet by administrators. It's true that the latter not infrequently *act* like they plan on meeting future acts of aggression against heterodox students with strictness. They'll pay the standard lip service to their schools' "values" of tolerance, freedom of speech, and the like. Yet it is difficult to find many instances in which disciplinary action is meted out to offending parties, much less action that involves anything like expulsion or arrests.

Shortly after Charles Murray was prevented from speaking at Middlebury College by disruptive students, Jim Trent of National Review Online wrote: "What amazes me about these riots and near riots on college campuses is that no one seems to be doing anything about it."

Indeed. There were professors present in the auditorium during Murray's visit who said not a word to the unruly students who refused to allow the invited guest to speak.

At California State University-Los Angeles, a conservative students' group on campus—Young Americans for Freedom (YAF)—arranged to have Ben Shapiro deliver a speech titled: "When Diversity Becomes a Problem." The students received threats and insults from other students and faculty alike. In short, they were branded "white supremacists."

Initially, the college charged them an astronomical fee for security, justifying the expenditure on the grounds that the presentation would be "controversial." Then, the college cancelled it altogether, suggesting that it be replaced with a "more inclusive event."

Administrators are doing little to nothing to protect their conservative and moderate students in an environment that is becoming increasingly dangerous for them. Students who actually are threatened or assaulted should press charges with the local police. State legislatures need to determine whether their laws are being violated on campuses. They must also see to it that appropriate penalties are affixed to what crimes are occurring against students because of their political views.

And, if these colleges are the recipients of federal funds, this funding should be withdrawn.

The situation at far too many places in the world of Higher Education has become inexcusable given the university's traditional mission to be a marketplace of ideas devoted to the pursuit and dissemination of knowledge. If administrators aren't going to act to rectify these injustices of their own accord, then legal authorities must compel them to do so.

Higher Miseducation

Math Is So...White?!

IF IT HADN'T already become obvious, it is now *painfully* obvious that leftists, particularly the agents of the Racism-Industrial-Complex (RIC), have become a parody of themselves.

The academic left never fails to take the lead in these matters. A professor of mathematics education at the University of Illinois, Rochelle Gutierrez, has recently claimed in a chapter that she contributed to an anthology designed for mathematics teachers that *math* is, in effect, "racist."

To be more precise, math promotes..."Whiteness." Gutierrez writes:

> *On many levels, mathematics itself operates as Whiteness. Who gets credit for doing and developing mathematics, who is capable in mathematics, and who is seen as part of the mathematical community is generally viewed as White.*

She elaborates:

> *School mathematics curricula, emphasizing terms like Pythagorean theorem and pi perpetuate a perception that mathematics was largely developed by Greeks and other Europeans.*

Moreover, "mathematics operates with unearned privilege in society, just like Whiteness."

Gutierrez laments that we regard mathematics "as if it is a natural reflection of the universe," occurring "outside of human influence," "encoding the universe with eternal truths, a natural order of things that should not be questioned."

Thus, "mathematics is viewed as a version of the world that is proper, separate from humans, where no emotions or agendas take place."

Mathematics becomes normative, the benchmark of clear thinking, due to "its perceived purity [.]"

Gutierrez maintains that this value-neutral, normative conception of mathematics has had "lasting" and negative "effects" on legions of people who are "not viewed as mathematical"—which is another way of saying that they are not viewed as intelligent.

"So many people," Gutierrez continues, "have experienced trauma, microaggressions from participating in math classrooms where the idea of being a successful person, being an intelligent person, is removing oneself from the context, not involving emotions, not involving the body, and being judged by whether one can reason abstractly."

Gutierrez's point here is that, "whether we recognize it or not, mathematics teaching is a highly political activity." This in turn means that "if teachers are unable to deconstruct the deficit messages circulating in society about themselves, their students, or public education," if they "situate the problem of learning in individual student motivation and ignore broader institutional and systemic inequities," then "they cannot successfully advocate for policies and practices that are research-based and ethically just."

Some thoughts:

First, Professor Gutierrez reveals in this essay that she is among the Initiated in contemporary leftism. It doesn't take long for those who pay any attention to them to recognize that academic leftists (sadly, a virtual redundancy) have a tendency to trade in jargon of a specific kind, buzz words which suggest, and seem designed to suggest, that their users are members of one and the same secret society of sorts. Gutierrez espouses several of them in just the few passages that are quoted here: "deconstruct," "Whiteness," "privilege," "institutional and systemic inequities," and, of course, "microaggressions."

And, of course, her insistence that *all* teaching, including and most notably the teaching of mathematics, is political, locates Gutierrez solidly among the Gnostics, distinguishing her as a Fellow Traveler in the eyes of her ideological ilk in the academy.

Second, it is also telling that the lingua franca of the contemporary academy in which Gutierrez has shown herself to be so fluent consists largely of highly abstract nouns. Ironically, it is precisely those leftists, like Professor Gutierrez, who are forever assuring us of the historically pernicious effects of the "privileged" position to which the West has allegedly elevated abstract thought that resort to abstraction the most.

It is leftists who appear the least interested in attending to any and all details that threaten to upset those of their theories—like the theory that mathematics "operates" as "Whiteness"—that are ideologically serviceable.

The conservative scholar Roger Scruton noted the peculiar characteristics of this esoteric manner of speaking, which he aptly calls "Newspeak."

> *The world of Newspeak [the world as it is envisioned by leftists, especially academic leftists, like Gutierrez] is a world of abstract forces, in which individuals are merely local embodiments of 'isms' that are revealed in them; hence, it is a world without [individual human] action.*

This being said, the world of Newspeak is most definitely not a world devoid of "movement. On the contrary, everything is in constant motion, swept onwards by the forces of progress, or impeded by the forces of reaction. There is no equilibrium, no stasis, [and] no rest in the world of Newspeak."

The eighteenth century philosopher David Hume too noted the benefits to be reaped from the use of abstract terms: "It is easy for a false hypothesis to maintain some appearance of truth, while it keeps wholly in generals" and "makes use of undefined terms [.]"

He added that "ideas, especially abstract ones, are naturally faint and obscure: the mind has but a slender hold of them…and when we have often employed any term, though without a distinct meaning, we are apt to imagine it has a determinate idea annexed to it."

In other words, Professor Gutierrez can maintain the ludicrous thesis that "mathematics operates as Whiteness" only because she "keeps" it "wholly in generals," as Hume says, only because she packages it in terms of the very kinds of abstractions against which she rails.

Finally, while Rochelle Gutierrez, judging from her press in conservative media, has generated quite the stir, her position on the issue of mathematics shouldn't come as a surprise to anyone who knows anything about the academic left.

For example, the now late Iris Marion Young claimed years ago that while it "poses as neutral and universal," "the ideal of a common humanity in which all can participate without regard to race, gender, religion, or sexuality…allows privileged groups to ignore their own group specificity" and facilitates the "disadvantage" at which "oppressed groups" find themselves.

The problem, as Young saw it, is that the ideals of "formal equality" and "assimilation" obscure group differences that need to be made explicit if "the dominant culture" is to recognize itself "for the first time as specific: as Anglo, European,

Christian, masculine, straight [.]"

Only then will patterns that "structure privilege and oppression" cease.

By way of the Newspeak of the left, *anything,* whether the delivery of mathematics or the ideals of color-blindness, formal opportunity, and assimilation, can be racialized and wielded as an indictment of European or white society.

But what the left either doesn't recognize or refuses to recognize is that the very ideals on behalf of which they advocate, like Equality, are themselves Eurocentric to the core. The ideas of natural or "human" rights, Democracy, liberalism, progressivism, and so forth are the intellectual artifacts, the inventory, as it were, of a specific civilization: the West.

If Gutierrez and Young and their ilk cared about consistency, they'd be forced to admit that what goes for mathematics and the like goes equally well for everything else. Racism, sexism, homophobia, Islamophobia, and xenophobia, like mathematics, all "operate" to facilitate Whiteness, for such *forces* are evil only if the Individual—another Eurocentric notion—transcends them. Thus, by promoting the idea that these things are wrong, one, paradoxically, promotes…Whiteness!

This, however, is a conclusion that the agents of the Racism-Industrial-Complex must fight to the death to avoid, for once admitted, *they* would have to die.

Jack Kerwick

Academics as a "Thought-Collective"

EVERYONE IS FAMILIAR with "peer-pressure."

Adults like to convince themselves that peer-pressure is a juvenile phenomenon, something to which only children and, especially, teenagers are subjected. Grown-ups, we assure ourselves, are sufficiently tough-minded and strong-willed. Unlike weaker, immature kids, we are individuals with the courage to go our own way—regardless of who thinks what.

This way of thinking is especially self-delusional in the case of contemporary academics, just those who, presumably, are sufficiently discerning to recognize that the ethos of their peers is far from a self-evident Truth.

Yet ideological conformity, or Groupthink, is more entrenched in academia than it is almost anywhere.

Academics tend to constitute what the Polish-Jewish philosopher of science Ludwik Fleck called a "thought collective." A thought collective is a community the members of which largely endorse the same ideas and share common manners of thinking and perceiving. "Thinking is a collective activity," Fleck wrote back in the 1930's. "Its product is a certain picture, which is visible only to anybody who takes part in this social activity, or a thought which is also clear to the members of the collective only."

In short: "What we do think and how we do see depends

on the thought-collective to which we belong."

Every thought-collective has a "collective mood" and a "thought style." The former produces the latter.

"The force which maintains the collective and unites its members," Fleck explains, "is derived from the community of the *collective mood*. This mood produces the readiness for an *identically directed perception, evaluation and use of what is perceived*, i.e. a common thought-style" (emphasis added).

In other words, the collective mood of a thought-collective binds its members by demanding of them the affirmation of common values and the thinking of common thoughts. Even the technical terminology of the "esoteric" circle of the thought-collective—its elite, the specialists, those who have achieved a greater degree of fluency in the discourse of the collective—have anything but the cold, value-neutral accuracy that they are supposed to possess. Quite the contrary: These terms have "a specific thought-charm," "a certain specific power," for they are "not only a name but a slogan."

That this is the case, Fleck says, is borne out readily enough by the widespread sense on the part of new members of an esoteric circle that joining it has "the value of the sacrament of initiation."

The "identically directed perception, evaluation and use of what is perceived" required for the solidarity among the members of a thought-collective is achieved through emotion-laden terms or "thought-charms." It as well obtained by way of the neglect and marginalization of those outside the collective.

Focusing on the contemporary state of the liberal arts and humanities, it doesn't take a stretch of the imagination to apply Fleck's theory of the thought-collective to academia. This thought-collective is marked by a distinctive manner of conceiving reality, what is commonly recognized by both its members as well as non-members as an ideologically *leftist* or "Politically Correct" orientation.

The dominant thought-collective of academics in the liberal arts (including the "social" sciences) is facilitated by way of a specialized idiom that reinforces conformity among its members while devaluing non-members. Here are some examples:

Social Justice: Academics tirelessly proclaim their commitment to *"social* justice"—never plain, traditional *justice.*

Equality/Inequality: There is no topic over which academics obsess more than this one. In fact, the fight for "social justice" *is* the fight against "inequalities" and/or for Equality. But by Equality, what the members of this thought-collective have in mind is a centrally-directed distribution of material and economic resources that comports with the ideal distribution of their imaginings.

Racism: For as much as this term is used by everyone these days, no one really knows what, if anything, it even means. While your average person is ready to equate it with a hatred for or a willingness to do bad to the members of another race, this is decidedly *not* what contemporary academics mean by this term.

"Racism" is used by the thought-collective of academics to denote a *subconscious* phenomenon limited (almost entirely) to *white people*. It is said to saturate the very institutions or "structures" (another thought-charm) of European or Western civilization. Thus, by this definition, even the most benevolent, well-meaning of whites is affected by "racism."

White Privilege: This is another weasel word that is all the rage among academics these days. "White privilege" denotes nothing. However, it is meant to reinforce the unsubstantiated, verifiably false charge that non-white peoples remain the targets of relentless "racism."

Whether an individual is rich or poor, successful or unsuccessful, virtuous or vicious, if he or she is white, then he or she enjoys an existence more "privileged" than any experienced by any other nonwhite person—however wealthy, powerful, famous, healthy, and even happy this nonwhite person may be.

Higher Miseducation

Do you see how this works? Whites are always guilty because of their unmerited "privilege" while nonwhites are always at a "disadvantage" that is just as unmerited.

And this brings us to our next thought-charmer.

The Disadvantaged: This abstraction refers to no one, though it is devised to imply that those, primarily nonwhites, who by any social index fare worse than whites do so because they are at a "disadvantage." *This* in turn is meant to suggest that their disadvantage has been imposed upon them by—who else?—the larger white society.

Sexism / Homophobia / Islamophobia / Transphobia / Xenophobia, etc.: Space constraints preclude a more thorough analysis here, but the bottom line is this: The thought-collective comprised of academics has created whole departments invested exclusively in promoting the fiction that the entirety of Western (European) civilization is responsible for the mistreatment of women, gays, Muslims, the trans-gendered, and, well, everyone other than white Christian men.

And while these "isms" and "phobias" have no *denotation*, this matters not, for the members of the thought-collective care only that they *connote* something really bad. As with "racism" and "white privilege," "sexism," "homophobia," and the like are said to reside within the very institutions and assumptions of Western societies.

This list of these "slogans" with their "thought charm" could be expanded indefinitely. For now, though, it should be clear that (most of) today's academics, far from being deep, curious thinkers, are in reality joint-members of a thought-collective.

Jack Kerwick

Academia's "New Civics" vs. Traditional American Civics

THE ELECTION OF Donald J. Trump to the office of the Presidency of the United States came as a body blow to leftists. Actually, such was their arrogance—their certitude that their candidate couldn't lose—that President Trump's victory hit them more like a sucker punch.

Students and their professors at colleges and universities from around the country participated in "cry-ins," entered "safe spaces," cancelled classes and examinations, and organized demonstrations.

While the rest of the country looked incredulously upon this spectacle of presumably educated adults protesting the legitimate election of America's 45th President, those of us who know a thing or two about the contemporary academic world were not in the least surprised by it.

And those academics who belong to the National Association of Scholars (NAS) know more than most.

The NAS recently released a report on the latest wave of anti-intellectualism to sweep the world of "higher education." In "Making Citizens: How American Universities Teach Civics," the NAS explains what it refers to as "the New Civics." The latter "redefines civics as progressive political activism."

While the New Civics styles itself "as an up-to-date version of volunteerism and good works," the reality is that it stems from "the radical program of the 1960's New Left [.]" Its "soft rhetoric" is designed to conceal its architects' ultimate goals.

First, they want to "repurpose higher education." Secondly, adherents of the New Left want nothing more than to make students into joint enterprisers in "'fundamentally transforming' America."

This dream of fundamental transformation that the left wants for students to make into a reality is fairly comprehensive. For starters, it involves "de-carbonizing the economy [.]" Yet it also involves "massively redistributing wealth, intensifying identity group grievance, curtailing the free market, expanding government bureaucracy, elevating international 'norms' over American Constitutional law, and disparaging our common history and ideals."

Although leftist academics disagree amongst themselves as to how to prioritize the items on this agenda, they are of one mind that "America must be transformed by 'systemic change' from an unjust, oppressive society to a society that embodies social justice."

The NAS report discloses *how* the New Civics plans to achieve its goals. It "hopes to accomplish" all of "this by teaching students that a good citizen is a radical activist…."

The New Civics "puts political activism at the center of everything that students do in college, including academic study, extra-curricular pursuits, and off-campus ventures."

A current feature of college life is what is called "service-learning." The NAS report finds that this all too often proves to be an "effort to divert students from the classroom to vocational training as community activists."

One major problem with "service-learning" is that it has "succeeded in capturing nearly all the funding that formerly supported the old civics." What "this means [is] that instead of teaching college students the foundations of law, liberty, and self-government, colleges teach students how to organize

Jack Kerwick

protests, occupy buildings, and stage demonstrations."

The authors of the NAS report concede that while protests, demonstrations, and occupations may be forms of "'civic engagement,'" they hardly constitute "a genuine substitute for learning how to be a full participant in our republic."

Case studies of the University of Colorado, Boulder (CU-Boulder), Colorado State University in Fort Collins (CSU), the University of Northern Colorado in Greeley (UNC), and the University of Wyoming in Laramie (UW) establish that its proponents are determined to implement the New Civics in "every college class regardless of subject."

In a preface to this study, Peter Wood, the President of the NAS, puts the point bluntly: "What is most new about the New Civics is that while it claims the name of civics, it is really a form of anti-civics." This is no hyperbole. Wood explains:

> *Civics in the traditional American sense meant learning about how our republic governs itself. The topics ranged from mastering simple facts, such as the branches of the federal government and the obligations of citizenship, to reflecting on the nature of Constitutional rights and the system of checks and balances that divide the states from the national government and the divisions of the national government from one another. A student who learns civics learns about voting, serving on juries, running for office, serving in the military, and all of the other key ways in which citizens take responsibility for their own government.*

Matters are dramatically otherwise with the so-called New Civics, which largely neglects these matters altogether. Here, "the largest preoccupation is getting students to engage in coordinated social action." It's true that this occasionally consists of "political protest," but more frequently it entails enlisting students in the service of promoting "progressive causes."

Wood cites illustrations of this phenomenon from the University of Colorado at Boulder where students have been encouraged do things like opening "dialogue between immigrants and native-born residents of Boulder County," march "in support of the United Farm Workers," and undermine "'gender binary' spaces in education."

It isn't just at the college level that civics has been replaced with activism. This has been occurring throughout our educational system since the New Left arose in the late 1960's. Those who belong to the NAS are not alone in recognizing the harm that the politicization of learning, the substitution of training in an ideology for a genuine education, has done to the citizenry. That being said, the National Association of Scholars is particularly deserving of praise for its tireless efforts to draw the public's attention to corruption within higher education.

This report on the "New Civics," or "anti-civics," is just its latest clarion call.

Jack Kerwick

From Higher Education to Political Indoctrination: Examples from the Front

PARENTS WHO PLAN on refinancing their homes in order to send their children off to college should instead consider encouraging them to specialize in a trade.

Speaking as a Ph.D. in philosophy who has spent the last 17 years teaching at the college level, I'm perhaps the last person from whom advice of this sort is expected. But it is precisely because of my familiarity with academia that I beseech the college bound and their enablers—I mean their supporters—to revisit their plans.

Whether one regards a post-secondary institution as a means to either a remunerative profession or a genuine education, the tragic fact of the matter is that the contemporary academic world is about as politicized a cultural institution as any.

More specifically, it is a bastion of Political Correctness, a decidedly leftist ideology that tolerates no competition.

For the last 11 years, Professor Duke Pesta, who is currently an associate professor of English at the University of Wisconsin Oshkosh, has taught literature at a range of colleges. At the outset of each semester, he would quiz his students on their knowledge of American and Western history. What he found is that the "overwhelming" number of them believed that slavery—an institution, mind you, that is as old as humanity itself, was practiced in virtually every society the planet over, and that lasted only some 87 years in the United States—was an exclusively American phenomenon.

"Most of my students could not tell me anything meaningful about slavery outside of America," Pesta told *The College Fix*. His students "are convinced that slavery was an American problem that more or less ended with the Civil War and they are very fuzzy about slavery prior to the Colonial era."

"Their entire education about slavery," he adds, "was confined to America."

Yet it isn't just students who display an astonishing ignorance of slavery. Over at Boston University, Saida Grundy, an Assistant Professor of sociology and African-American Studies, tweeted that slavery is "a white people…thing."

Grundy didn't stop there. She asks: "is white people's new deflection from dealing with slavery that 'all races have had slaves' thing? is this the new '#AllLivesMatter'?"

Professor Grundy added other enlightening tweets:

"for the record, NO race outside of Europeans had a system that made slavery a *personhood* instead of temporary condition;

"there is also no race except Europeans who kidnapped and transported human beings in order to enslave them and their offspring for life;

"before Europeans invented it as such, slavery was not a condition that was de facto inherited from parent to child."

In case white folks couldn't follow the thrust of her rant, Grundy offers a summation of her sophisticated position:

"in other words, deal with your white sh*t, white people. slavery is a *YALL* thing."

In addition to assigning blame for slavery solely to white

Europeans, Grundy claimed that "white masculinity" is "THE problem for america's colleges."

Over at the University of Pittsburgh, students who were distributing pro-Donald Trump materials were harassed and attacked. The Trump supporters were accused of backing a "racist" candidate who espouses "hate speech." They were greeted by chants of "f**k the white male patriarchy" and, eventually, physical aggression.

One of the victims said that "my campus shouldn't be a place where my friends and I are fearful for having opposing opinions."

These students were accosted by other students. Students elsewhere, however, have had professors with which to contend.

At the University of California at Los Angeles (UCLA), a political science professor, Michael Chwe, wrote in a blog post for Princeton University Press that "the danger to democracy itself" is posed by "Trump supporters [.]" This "danger" is "real and must be confronted." Chwe maintains that Trump and his supporters are "the greatest danger to democracy since World War II, even perhaps since the Civil War [.]"

Chwe thinks that had "we" done "a better and earlier job with confronting, as opposed to accommodating, white and male privilege…we might not have reached this situation [the Trump phenomenon]." "We" must set our sights on "combatting" these forms of "privilege" now, though, if we hope to divert "democracy away from self-destruction."

And it isn't just faculty in the humanities and liberal arts that can't resist injecting their politics into the classroom.

A *math* professor at Mount Holyoke College, an all-female school, was recently captured on video launching into an anti-Trump/pro-Clinton tirade in class. While he never referred to either candidate by name, Peter Rosnick's choice for president was plain. This election, Rosnick said, is the "scariest" that he's ever witnessed. He told his students that they should "vote for someone who thinks women are full and capable and responsible and intelligent beings who should not be the object of, um, should not be objectified."

Rosnick also prescribed his students to vote "for whoever you want, but vote for somebody who respects the fact that this is a country built on immigrants—that this is a country that couldn't, that wouldn't be what it is if it wasn't for bringing immigrants into our nation and respecting them and respecting what they bring to our country."

At least one of Rosnick's students was less than enthused over his proselytizing efforts. Speaking on condition of anonymity, this student told *The College Fix* that she found "it highly inappropriate for a math teacher to use my class time to try to tell me who to vote for."

Indeed.

But this, unfortunately, is hardly an anomaly in 2016. Thus, parents should think hard before divesting themselves of tens and tens of thousands of dollars so that their children can become targets of political indoctrination.

Jack Kerwick

Profile in Courage at Duke University

THAT, OF ALL people, Barack Obama recently received the Kennedy Library's "Profile in Courage" award proves that the latter has about as much to do with recognizing courage as the Nobel Peace Prize, of which the former President was also a recipient, has to do with honoring peace.

This is not meant to be a knock against Obama. Rather, it is an observation that no unprejudiced spectator of the contemporary American scene could fail to make. The stone-cold truth is that there is utterly nothing courageous about being a self-avowed "progressive," a Politically Correct leftist, in today's Western world.

And Obama is nothing if not a leftist.

No, neither Obama nor his ideological ilk in Washington D.C., Hollywood, the (fake) news media, and academia display a scintilla of courage in their public lives. Real bravery, as all of us teach our children, is a matter of resisting groupthink—or "peer pressure," as we call it when referring to youth. Real courage consists in daring to challenge the prevailing ideological orthodoxy—or "what's popular," as the kids call it.

There are indeed people who are deserving of an award affirming courage. One such person is Paul Griffiths, a divinity professor at Duke University. Professor Griffiths, whose area of specialization is Catholic theology, is a prolific writer and scholar. He has been teaching at Duke since 2008.

He will not be returning to his position in the fall.

In February, an invitation was emailed to the divinity school faculty encouraging them to attend a two-day seminar on "racial equity" training. Anathea Portier-Young, an Associate Professor of the Old Testament, replied enthusiastically: "Those who have participated in the training have described it as transformative, powerful, and life-changing," she wrote. "We recognize that it is a significant commitment of time; we also believe that it will have great dividends for our community," she said.

Griffiths disagreed. He copied all of his colleagues on his response. "I exhort you not to attend this training," he began. "Don't lay waste your time by doing so. It'll be, I predict with confidence, intellectually flaccid: there'll be bromides, clichés, and amen-corner rah-rahs in plenty. When (if) it gets beyond that, its illiberal roots and totalitarian tendencies will show."

Griffiths concluded: "Events of this sort are definitively anti-intellectual."

Of course, Griffiths is entirely correct. "Events of this sort" are most definitely, always, profoundly anti-intellectual. They are instruments designed to totalize the groupthink, the religious-like dogma, of the academy. That Griffiths dared to defy the orthodoxy, that he dared to openly resist the "cool kids," and that he undoubtedly knew what was to come next earns him a Profile in Courage award.

The Divinity school Dean, Elain Heath, responded to all faculty. She didn't mention Griffiths by name. However, it was clear to all that it was he who she had in mind when she condemned the "inappropriate and unprofessional" nature of "mass emails" containing "disparaging statements—including arguments ad hominem" that are intended "to humiliate or undermine individual colleagues or groups of colleagues with whom we disagree."

To insure that her point wasn't lost upon anyone, Heath was explicit:

> *The use of mass emails to express racism, sexism, and other forms of bigotry is offensive and unacceptable, especially in a Christian institution.*

While Dean Heath reportedly attempted to meet with Griffiths in person, this never came to pass. Subsequently, Griffiths sent out another mass email. The subject line read: "intellectual freedom and institutional discipline." According to *The News and Observer,* Griffiths revealed to his colleagues that he had become the "targets" of *two* disciplinary proceedings. The first involves a harassment complaint filed by Portier-Young, the Old Testament professor who couldn't rave enough about the "racial equity training." The other has led Dean Heath to ban him from all faculty meetings and deprive Griffiths of funding for future research and traveling expenses.

As Griffiths sees it, Heath's actions are "reprisals" against him, means by which she can "discipline" him for articulating views with which she disagrees. "Duke University," Griffiths stated, "is now a place in which too many thoughts can't be spoken and too many disagreements remain veiled because of fear."

This being the case, Griffiths urged a "renunciation of fear-based discipline to those who deploy and advocate it, and its replacement with confidence in speech."

Professor Griffiths has resigned from his position at Duke, effective next fall.

Griffiths richly deserves an award that recognizes his bravery. To be fair, however, so too does his colleague, Thomas Pfau, a professor of English and German, warrant recognition for having come to Griffiths' defense.

Pfau commented:

> *Having reviewed Paul Griffiths' note several times, I find nothing in it that could even remotely be said to 'express racism, sexism, and other forms of bigotry.' To suggest anything of the sort strikes me as either gravely imperceptive or as intellectually dishonest.*

Pfau added:

> *I also felt that differences of opinion, however stark, ought to be respected and engaged, rather than being used for the purpose of moral recrimination.*

Pfau describes Griffiths as:

> *…one of the pre-eminent theologians working in the United States today and a vital resource for students and colleagues engaged in rigorous theological reflection here at Duke.*

He claims to "profoundly regret" Griffiths' decision to part ways with Duke, and told him that he believed that it was a "mistake."

Evidently, though, it is too late.

Thanks to Griffiths' willingness to speak up, *The New York Times,* of all places, now depicts Duke as "a new battleground" in the fight over "political correctness." Whether the events that Professor Griffiths set in motion materialize into a larger battle, and whether any other academics, besides Professor Pfau, follow his example remain to be seen.

Two things are for certain: Griffiths acted heroically.

And Barack Obama has never shown a fraction of the courage that Paul Griffiths has shown.

Jack Kerwick

For Your Typical Academic, Reason Is "Whiteness"

TO HEAR THE contemporary professoriate tell it, it isn't just mathematics that promotes "whiteness."

John Caputo and George Yancy are philosophers who agree that reason itself is "a function of whiteness." In 2015, Yancy, a black man, interviewed Caputo, a white man, for a series appearing in the *New York Times*. In "Looking 'White' in the Face," Yancy remarks that "the task of engaging race or whiteness in philosophy has been taken up almost exclusively by nonwhite philosophers."

Whiteness, Yancy maintains, "is *a site of privilege* that makes it invisible to many white philosophers." Moreover, "some white philosophers would rather avoid thinking about how their own whiteness raises deeper philosophical questions about identity, power, and hegemony, as this raises the question of personal responsibility."

Professor Caputo agrees: "'White,'" he says, "is of the utmost relevance to philosophy...and 'we' white philosophers cannot ignore it [.]" Elaborating, he states: "White is not 'neutral.' 'Pure' reason is lily white, as if white is not a color or is closest to the purity of the sun, and everything else is 'colored.'"

What all of this implies is that whatever "is not white is not rational." So, "white" is indeed "philosophically relevant and needs to be philosophically critiqued [.]"

Caputo thinks that "racism arises from a profound fear of the other" and that professional white philosophers tend not to write about "racism…in part because of a certain thoughtlessness [.]"

To be more thoughtful on this score, Caputo suggests that Yancy and other non-whites "interrupt" their white counterparts "and ask, 'To what extent is everything you just said a function of being white?'"

In summary, these two professional philosophers, one black, the other white, agree that "reason," at least as philosophers understood it, is a "function of whiteness." As such, it promotes "racism."

Being a professional philosopher myself, I find this exchange at once comical, exacerbating, and, ultimately, tragic. It is its comedic dimension, though, that I'd like to focus upon here.

First, although they clearly style themselves envelope-pushers, the reality is that on this topic of race and racism (as well as on many others) the overwhelming majority of contemporary academic philosophers are indistinguishable from Yancy and Caputo, who are in turn ideologically indistinguishable from one another.

That is to say, the overwhelming majority of contemporary academic philosophers, like Yancy and Caputo, are doctrinaire leftists.

Second, as was noted above in focusing on the esoteric-like vocabulary in which Yancy and Caputo trade, in listening to (or reading) their dialogue one could be forgiven for thinking that one is getting a glimpse into a secret society or cult. Both the terms peddled by contemporary academic philosophers as well as their obsessive preoccupation with the racialization of all things supply a window into the worldview of the Initiated.

Finally, and most importantly, this worldview shared by

Yancy, Caputo, and, to repeat, the vast majority of academic philosophers (and Humanities faculty generally) is ultimately *incoherent*. Of course, its proponents can't recognize this fact because they haven't the courage to abandon their "thoughtlessness," to borrow Yancy's and Caputo's term. They haven't the courage to think through the implications of their position.

> (1) While Caputo and Yancy are busy equating philosophy or "reason" with "whiteness" and sweating over a solution to what they obviously take to be a very big problem, they fail to realize that in proposing as the remedy a "critique" of "whiteness," they in effect propose to…strengthen their problem! To critique is to *rationally* critique. If reason is a species of whiteness, then to exercise reason—even in a critique of reason—is to reinforce whiteness.
>
> (2) If reason is whiteness, then so too is the English language, the language in which Caputo and Yancy speak and write and in which the paper—the *New York Times*—for which Yancy conducts his interviews of professional philosophers is printed.

So too is *America* the equivalent of whiteness, for it was named by those whites who settled it and in honor of the (white) Italian explorer, Amerigo Vespucci.

So too is the Constitution and the Declaration of Independence tantamount to whiteness, for they were written by white men—Southern, slave-holding, white men—and sanctioned by white men.

So too, then, is the *free speech* that Yancy and Caputo take for granted a product of whiteness.

Higher Miseducation

So too is the idea of the University, where Yancy and Caputo are paid to write and lecture about whiteness, a species of whiteness, for it is part of the legacy of the European world.

So too, then, is the notion of *Academic Freedom* that Yancy and Caputo prize saturated in whiteness.

So too is the ideal of *Equality* that Yancy and Caputo cherish "a function of whiteness."

So too is the ideal of *Diversity* that Yancy and Caputo value a matter of whiteness.

In his critique of whiteness, Caputo refers to "the Cartesian ego cogito and Kant's transcendental consciousness" as "white male Euro-Christian construction(s)." He is referring to the theories of two of Western civilization's greatest thinkers, Rene Descartes and Immanuel Kant, respectively. Though their conceptions of personal identity are not *explicitly* Christian, they would have been inconceivable had it not been for the "Euro-Christian" tradition from which, as Caputo rightly notes, Descartes and Kant both hail.

This is to say that Descartes and Kant both affirmed *the Individual*. Kant in particular grounded his case for the inviolable dignity of all persons in his theory of "transcendental consciousness," the capacity, unique to persons, for rational thought.

The point is this: The very idea that it is a *problem* that reason is a function of whiteness is *itself a function of whiteness*.

If whiteness promotes "Euro-Christian hegemony" over non-whites and non-Christians, and whiteness is, then, an evil to be eliminated, this could only be because the Individual has inviolable moral worth, an inherent dignity that transcends considerations of race, gender, ethnicity, and so forth. Yet the Individual is to Euro-Christian thought what apple pie is to America.

The Individual is "a function of whiteness."

We've now come full circle. The Yancys and Caputos of

the present academy are the proverbial dog chasing its tail: In order to critique "whiteness" they must affirm "whiteness." To put it even more clearly, only those who affirm "whiteness" could have a problem with "whiteness," and the solution to "whiteness" must itself be "a function of whiteness."

But I suppose that in identifying the self-contradiction at the heart of their worldview and insisting upon rational consistency, the Yancys and Caputos would accuse me of advancing "whiteness."

"Social Justice" Over Truth: The University's New Mission

JONATHAN HAIDT, A professor of social psychology at New York University, argued in a recently published essay that while its traditional "telos" (end or goal) has been *truth,* within the last few decades the university has assumed another: Social Justice.

The university, however, can only have one telos.

The conflict between these two goals has raged for decades, Haidt claims. Last year, though, it became unmanageable when student groups at 86 universities and colleges around the country issued "demands" to administrators, demands for Social Justice that, by and large, were met.

The following statement is posted at BlackLiberationCollective.org:

"We demand at the minimum, Black students and Black faculty to be reflected by the national percentage of Black folk in the state and the country.

We demand free intuition for Black and indigenous students.

We demand a divestment from prisons and an investment in communities."

A statement of "principles" follows. The Black Liberation Collective (BLC) opposes "anti-Blackness;" "sexism;" "ableism;" "capitalism;" "White privilege;" "inequality;" and "heteronormativity." It rejects as well *non-violence* considered as a *principle* in contradistinction to a *tactic*.

"Anti-Black racism is woven in the fabric of our global society," says the BLC. "When social systems are racialized by white supremacy, whiteness becomes the default of humanity and Blackness is stripped of its humanity, becoming a commodity, becoming disposable."

The BLC is "anti-sexist" insofar as it affirms "the value of all Black women's lives whether cisgender, transgender, or genderqueer." In addition to rejecting "Eurocentric beauty standards that are made to lessen the beauty of Black women and Black women's features," being "anti-sexist" also means realizing that "police brutality, the prison industrial system, school to prison pipeline" and the like are aspects of "structural racism" that affect black women as much as they impact black men.

Black liberation entails "queer liberation" and "trans liberation." "We also seek to destroy the heteronormative norms that dehumanize Black queer people," the BLC asserts. The "homophobia" within "the Black community" comes by way of "the same hands responsible for white supremacy."

Presumably, "transphobia" within the black community is also a legacy of white supremacy. In cooperation with "cissexism" and "the gender binary," "transphobia" has "been used as a means of invalidating and erasing our trans+ family members." The BLC pledges to "eliminate" such systemic biases.

These Social Justice Warriors (SJWs) are staunch opponents of "the capitalist notions of infinite profit, homogenized markets, and a privatized means of production." Capitalism, they insist, "is the economic system" that's been "used to justify" the "oppression," "marginalization," and "exploitation" of blacks.

Nor is the solution to this "oppression" to be found in supporting black-owned businesses. The BLC explains that "we cannot adopt the patriarchal, exploitative tools of our oppressors as we seek liberation." Rather, the solution is to "dismantle anti-

Black capitalist corporations that benefit from our oppression."

It isn't only the "capitalist corporations" that these students want destroyed. They demand as well "the eradication of all institutional practices and policies that discriminate against the black community" and "the removal of all federal, state, and local government officials who do not abide by our principles."

"The State and all its institutions that deny Black humanity and Black agency must be dismantled and replaced with those that produce Black liberty."

Concerning its attitude toward America, the BLC is clear: "This country was built to systematically oppress groups of people, and the Black Liberation Collective will not stand for it."

Haidt misspeaks in characterizing 2015 as the year when the university experienced a crisis of identity, an unmanageable conflict of goals. To judge from the vast majority of liberal arts, humanities, and social sciences departments, Social Justice long ago eclipsed truth as the raison d'etre of the academy. Interestingly, it is these SJW demands from last year that bear this out.

Perhaps it is because I've spent the last couple of decades in the academy in the capacity of both student and faculty that I may be more privy to this than are some others, but it's painfully obvious that these student activists did not come up with these demands on their own. If they didn't have their professors actually write the demands for them, then the Black Liberation Collective unquestionably derived the concepts and language of their statement of demands from their mentors.

To put it bluntly, one must attend college, major in the liberal arts and humanities, and study under far left professors in order to think in the terms that are characteristic of Social Justice Warriors.

Leftist ideologues are training their students to bend the university to their will. This is the first point. There is, though, another, a rich irony that is lost upon these self-styled radicals.

Jack Kerwick

For all of their bluster over "systemic racism" and "structural white supremacy," i.e. phenomena that are omnipresent and, hence, largely unconscious, these black students, their white collaborators, and *their professors* fail to realize that their thinking (for lack of a better term) on these issues is about as *Eurocentric* as one can get. The "critical race theory" to which the BLC subscribe is a version of Marxism, the philosophical vision of a 19th century German-Jewish man. The Marxist tradition within which they are enmeshed was fleshed out over a span of generations by mostly white heterosexual men.

But there's more to it than this.

The idea that "racism," "sexism," "homophobia," "transphobia," "ableism," and the like against which SJWs rail are evils to be defeated is itself peculiar to the moral traditions of European civilization. If these "isms" and "phobias" are immoral it can only be because those who are guilty of them fail to judge *the individual* as an individual. Color, gender, sexual orientation, ability, and so forth are neither constitutive of nor essential to the moral identity of the individual—but *only if* the framework of the doctrine of individualism is accepted.

Yet this conception of the sacrosanct individual is as Eurocentric as the proverbial "apple pie" is American.

The Social Justice Warriors' intellectual landscape is as much a European "colony" as was any West African country in the 19th or early 20th centuries. Those in the Black Liberation Collective have most definitely internalized the modes of thought of their "oppressor."

Now, they would have been well aware of all this had they received a genuine education in college rather than a training in Social Justice.

Higher Miseducation

If Student Protesters Were Consistent—But They're Not

AS I'VE NOTED in the past, the student (and faculty-endorsed) protests transpiring on college campuses throughout the land ultimately amount to nothing more or less than an anti-white campaign.

Whether the protesters and their leftist supporters recognize the inexorable logic of their demands, it points toward nothing short of the "fundamental transformation" of America and Western civilization itself.

And insofar as Western civilization is the house that Europeans, i.e. whites, built, this fundamental transformation that militant leftists wish to visit upon it can only amount to a purging of every last vestige of this legacy.

At Princeton University, black student-protesters and their white allies have gotten the administration to consider eradicating references to Woodrow Wilson, the "progressive" who, despite having served as president of both the United States and Princeton University, held racially regressive views.

At Yale University, student activists, including Dante de Blasio, son of Mayor Bill de Blasio of New York City, are in the process of pressuring administrators to change the name of one of its colleges that is named after John C. Calhoun—an apologist for slavery. Dante's father "absolutely" supports his son's efforts.

Perhaps these aggrieved students *and* their faculty allies, like their fellow travelers in the larger culture, are genuinely oblivious to their own inconsistencies. Or maybe they know exactly what they're doing. Either way, there is no circumventing the fact that if it is "racially insensitive" to blacks to name buildings after Wilson and Calhoun, then there is no getting around the following.

(1) For starters, it isn't just references to Wilson that should be purged from Princeton University; *Princeton University* should itself be purged. There would've been no College of New Jersey (subsequently renamed Princeton University) had it not been for Jonathan Belcher, a New Jersey governor whose efforts resulted in the establishment of this institution.

 Belcher, though, owned slaves.

 A one-time merchant, Belcher trafficked in slaves, and on one of his trips to England, he presented as a gift to Electress Sophia an Indian slave.

 How, we must ask, can we expect for these poor black students at Princeton to attend this most prestigious of the world's institutions of higher learning knowing that it was founded by a slave owner?! How can we expect American Indian students to do the same?!

(2) But it isn't just Princeton that must be abolished. So too must we eradicate most of America's elite universities—including Yale, where Mayor de Blasio's biracial son is forced to live under the daily oppression of attending a college named after a defender of slavery.

 As black author Craig Steven Wilder notes in his *Ebony and Ivy,* many of these institutions depended for their daily functioning upon slave labor.

(3) In his full-throated defense of his son, Mayor de Blasio insisted that his son would have to feel uncomfortable attending Yale's Calhoun College, because his son is of "African" descent.

Yet "African," like "Africa," is racially insensitive: "Africa" derives from "Afri"—a Latin name devised for referencing the inhabitants of what is today known as Africa. Latin was a *European* language. The boundaries of Africa have expanded as Europeans (whites) have discovered the land mass of the continent.

So, by the logic of student-protesters, shouldn't de Blasio's characterization of his son as being of "African" descent be treated as offensive? Isn't such a characterization a painful reminder to blacks of their ancestors' encounters with Europeans, of the omnipresence of "white privilege?"

(4) Yet if "Africa" is offensive, "African-*American*" is doubly offensive, for America, we should never forget, was named after *Amerigo Vespucci,* a European—a white—explorer.

(5) "America," then, is another word that should go the way of the names of Woodrow Wilson, John Calhoun, and others, for "America" reminds people of color, particularly Native Americans, of the "White Supremacy" that they have daily been forced live under for centuries.

(6) Then again, "Native American" is racially insensitive as well: The implication here is that America had always existed, but the "natives" were here *first*. The problem with this is that *there were no "Americas" before the Europeans invented them.* "Native American" is a

Eurocentric construct through and through.

(7) Of course, if we do retire the word "America," we do so at the risk of offending *women,* for America is a *feminine* term. That such a move may be racially enlightened in no way precludes it from being "sexist."

(8) Obviously, if references to Wilson and Calhoun are racially insensitive, then references to George Washington and Thomas Jefferson have got to be blood curdling. Washington and Jefferson, after all, were massive slave owners. If we are to provide a safe space to non-whites, then every site, city, and memorial designed to commemorate these men must be erased.

This, it should go without saying, applies equally as well to all of America's founders who traded in slaves or otherwise entertained thoughts that fail to satisfy the constraints of contemporary racial orthodoxy.

(9) In connection to this last point, it is imperative that both the *Declaration of Independence* and the *Constitution* go the way of the names of Wilson and Calhoun.

Consider: How can we expect racial minorities to experience anything but unmitigated suffering knowing that their fellow citizens claim to revere documents that were endorsed by not a single person of color? Worse, these are documents endorsed by slave owners who regarded blacks as inferior to whites!

In the interest of racial sensitivity, the Declaration and Constitution must go.

(10) The American flag, a flag that flew over slavery, segregation, the mistreatment of Native American—I mean "indigenous"—persons, etc. must go.

(11) "Racism," "sexism," and the like are also racially insensitive. This claim will doubtless strike many as patently false, even bizarre. But it's true all of the same.

"Racism"—meaning (presumably) the mistreatment of an individual on the basis of race or color—is regarded as a moral evil precisely because it is held that the individual's worth transcends such morally irrelevant characteristics as race or color. However, *this* notion of *the individual*—let's call it individualism—is, well, *Eurocentric*: The moral doctrine of individualism took flight in and imbued the West before it spread to other lands and peoples with which the West came into contact.

The very word "racism" (and, by implication, "sexism," "homophobia," etc.) should go the way of the name of Woodrow Wilson, for it accentuates the dominance of the Eurocentric ideal of individualism.

(12) If Columbus Day is offensive or racially insensitive because it celebrates the European subjugation of the indigenous peoples of what would become the Americas, then other holidays that inescapably call to mind the Europeanization of the Americas must also be erased.

Christmas and Easter remind racial minorities of their oppression by reminding them of the religion—Christianity—of their oppressors. Ditto for Saints Patrick and Valentine Days. Thanksgiving is a reminder of the suffering that indigenous peoples endured as a consequence of Europeans' discovery of "the New World," as is Independence Day.

If student-protesters (and leftists generally) were consistent, they would be following this course.

But then again, logical consistency as an ideal they will probably dismiss as but another Eurocentric imposition.

Higher Miseducation

Trinity College Professor Says to Whites: "Let Them F**king Die!"

TRINITY COLLEGE IN Hartford, Connecticut is another fine illustration of the contemporary state of Higher Education. Johnny Eric Williams, a professor in its sociology department, is among the reasons why it enjoys this distinction.

On June 18, Williams—a black man—posted some blatantly anti-white remarks on his Facebook wall. Supposedly, after they went viral, Trinity and Williams were besieged with threats. Such was the alleged intensity and nature of the threats that administrators closed campus on the day of June 21.

Williams, for his part, maintains that he never meant for his remarks to be made public and that he was deliberately *misconstrued* by "conservative" sites.

You be the judge of this.

Below are two of Williams' posts from June 18. The first reads:

> It is past time for the racially oppressed to do what people who believe themselves to be 'white' will not do, put [an] end to the vectors of their destructive mythology of whiteness and their white supremacy system. #LetThemFuckingDie

And then there was the second:

Jack Kerwick

> *I'm fed the fuck up with self identified 'white's' daily violence directed at immigrants, Muslims, and sexual and racially oppressed people. The time is now to confront these inhuman assholes and end this now.*

On June 16, Williams shared on his page an article from the *Medium*. The essay's title is: *Let Them Fucking Die*.

The author, "Son of Baldwin," prefaces his own remarks with a quotation from a *Fusion* piece that references the mass shooting of Republican Congressman Steve Scalise and his colleagues in Alexandria, Virginia. The article notes "the irony" that Scalise, a person who "kept company with racists" and "white supremacists" and who is "one of the most anti-LGBTQ politicians in Washington," "may owe his life to a queer black woman."

Son of Baldwin expresses his frustration over what this episode "symbolizes." He asks: "What does it mean, in general, when victims of bigotry save the lives of bigots?"

The author launches into a rant that, in addition to being replete with lies, fallacies, and inaccuracies, suffers from a painfully conspicuous lack of originality. We have all heard this tirade before, tirelessly, for decades. It is the cardinal dogma of what I have elsewhere referred to as "Blackism," precisely that ideology designed to grant instant racial "authenticity" to any and all blacks who affirm it:

Blacks are perpetual victims of perpetual White Oppression.

Son of Baldwin is clear as to the course of action that blacks who are in a position to help white "bigots" should take. His position is boldfaced type:

"Let. Them. Fucking. Die."

But don't *just* do this. Blacks should "smile a bit" when they let white "bigots" die, for they "have done the universe a great service."

Higher Miseducation

And in case there is any ambiguity as to when, exactly, blacks should allow white "bigots" to die, Son of Baldwin tries his best to dispel it in advance.

"If you see them drowning," "in a burning building," "teetering on the edge of a cliff," or if "their ships are sinking," "their planes are crashing," or "their cars are skidding," blacks should smile as they let these white "bigots" *die*.

Bear in mind that while Son of Baldwin's focus on white *bigots* would seem to suggest that he is not referring to all white people, it is a certitude to anyone familiar with Blackist newspeak, the rhetoric of "white supremacy," "institutional racism," "white supremacy" and the like—rhetoric, not incidentally, that both Son of Baldwin and Johnny Eric Williams espouse—that *all white people* are "bigoted."

Son of Baldwin underscores this interpretation when he writes about "white/cisgender/heterosexuals who practice bigotry (or *do not believe they practice bigotry even when they do*)" (emphasis added) [.]"

This is article that Professor Williams shared.

Ever since Williams became the focal point of this controversy, he has maintained that he does not endorse allowing *individual* whites to die. Rather, it is for the death of a *system* of "white supremacy" that he calls.

"I'm calling for the death of a system, white supremacy, not the death of white people."

The President of Trinity College, Joanne Berger-Sweeney, condemned Williams' use of the hashtag, "LetThemFuckingDie," as "reprehensible and, at the very least, in poor judgment." She added that, "No matter its intent, it goes against our fundamental values as an institution [.]"

Before proceeding further, she has turned the matter over to the Dean of the Faculty to determine whether any college "procedures or policies were broken."

Two Connecticut politicians, Republican House Leader

Themis Klarides and state Senator George Logan, both Trinity graduates, wrote a letter to Berger-Sweeney imploring her to terminate Williams immediately. "We are calling upon the school to immediately, and permanently, remove Mr. Williams from the ranks of the school's faculty," they state.

Perhaps Professor Williams is sincere when he insists that it is not the demise of individual whites, but, rather, that of a system that he wants to see die. Judging from the quality, both stylistic and substantive, of his social media posts, this is a distinct possibility. It is a distinct possibility that Williams is genuinely as intellectually inept as someone would have to be not to recognize that, grammatically and logically, his posts can only be read as a call for allowing white "bigot*s*," "ignorant asshole*s*," i.e. a *plurality* of beings, not a single "system," to die.

The other option is that Williams is a coward and a liar who is now retreating from his initial position because of the backlash to it. Williams very well may be receiving the shock of his life in being made to realize that it isn't just black leftist SJWs that can get angry, that when people understandably think that someone is calling for their deaths, they will call for the same in return.

At any rate, decent people must condemn the threats of violence against Williams that are now allegedly being made against him. I for one won't even call for his termination. This, though, is only because Williams is but a symptom of a much larger system that has long since gone to the bad.

For sure, there remain many committed college instructors who care deeply about supplying their students with a genuine liberal arts education. And, to be fair, many, possibly most, of these are liberal-left. Yet, regrettably, the Johnny Williams of the academy are legion. The only difference between Williams and the untold numbers of humanities professors at colleges and universities throughout the country is that Williams got caught for expressing his anti-white vision.

Removing him would be like removing one cockroach from an infestation and thinking that the problem is solved.

The pressure that is now being brought upon Williams must be brought by the public upon the whole Academic Industrial Complex, for Williams' view is but a variant of the intellectually vapid and morally toxic ideology that dominates academia today.

Jack Kerwick

University of New Hampshire "Language Guide"

IF THERE REMAINED any doubts that academia is among the most thoughtless places in the cosmos, the University of New Hampshire just put them to rest once and for all.

The breathtaking Political Correctness embodied by UNH's recently released, "Bias-Free Language Guide" (BFLG), proves that higher education has become a one-dimensional caricature of itself. Indeed, right-wing reactionaries couldn't have done a better job in calling attention to the intellectual and moral shallowness, the remarkable lack of seriousness—or is it the remarkable abundance of *deadly* seriousness?—of academia.

And before anyone objects that the entire academic establishment shouldn't be judged on the basis of the actions of one school, it should be borne in mind that the *zeitgeist* expressed by UNH's latest de facto speech code *is* one and the same left-wing orthodoxy that has long achieved a stranglehold over the university.

The BFLG "is meant to serve as a starting point" in rethinking "terms related to age, race, class, ethnicity, nationality, gender, ability, sexual orientation and more" for the purpose of promoting "inclusive excellence in our campus community." In short, words that are infected with "bias" are "problematic" or "outdated;" those that are alleged to be "bias-free" are "preferred."

"People of advanced age" and "old people" are preferred. Terms like "older people," "elders," "seniors," and "senior citizen" are problematic and outdated.

Yes, believe it or not, "'old people' has been reclaimed by some older activists who believe the standard wording of old people lacks the stigma of the term 'advanced age.'" Moreover, the term "old people" also halts "the euphemizing of age." The latter is bad because in "euphemizing," we assume that "age is a negative."

"Poor person" and "person from the ghetto" are problematic and outdated. In contrast, "person who lacks advantages that others have" and "low economic status related to a person's education, occupation and income" are preferable.

Wow. If "poor person" is now a Politically Incorrect term, then it would appear that no word is safe.

Indeed: Even use of the word "homeless" reflects insensitivity on the part of the user. The BFLG explains that "homeless" "reduces the person to being defined by their housing rather than as a person first [.]"

Instead, "homeless" should give way to "person-experiencing homelessness."

"Obese" and "overweight" are offensive descriptors: the former is "the medicalization of size" while the latter is "arbitrary." Even "fat" is on its way to being preferable to either of these terms, for some "people of size"—the preferred term of choice—and "their allies" have "reclaimed" it.

"Non-disabled" is preferred to "able-bodied" and "normal."

"Person who is blind/visually impaired" is preferable to "blind person."

"U.S. citizen" or "resident of the U.S." is preferable to "American," for the latter "usually...fails to recognize South America."

"Foreigners" should be rejected in favor of "international people."

"Illegal alien" and "illegal" fail to affirm the humanity of those in question. But even "undocumented immigrant or worker," though generally preferable to the alternative, isn't wholly successful in recognizing "the person's humanity first."

"Sexual preference" is bad because it suggest that "being gay or lesbian is voluntary and therefore 'curable.'" On the other hand, "sexual orientation" and "sexual identity" are good.

"Homosexual" is out; "gay, lesbian, same gender-loving (SGL)" is in.

Alternative "lifestyle" is unacceptable in that it has been "used by anti-gay extremists to denigrate lesbian, gay, bisexual and transgender lives." "LGBTQ" is the only appropriate term here.

"Parenting" and "nurturing" are "non-gendered" activities. Thus, only if "gender is specifically implied" is it permissible to use the otherwise problematic terms of "mothering" and "fathering."

"Opposite sex" is offensive and insensitive. "*Other* sex" is more inclusive.

These are just *some* of the revisions to our language that the BFLG suggests. It also identifies a number of "micro-aggressions" like the "micro-assault," the "micro-insult," and the "micro-invalidation." A micro-assault is what the guide refers to as a "verbal attack." The example used is that of one person who, upon encountering another "using a mobile chair for long distance travel," questions the latter about his or her ability to walk.

This is a micro-assault.

A micro-insult is "a form of verbal or silent demeaning through insensitive comments or behavior," and a micro-invalidation consists in "degrading a person's wholeness through making false assumptions about the other's ability, causing a sense of invalidation."

UNH President, Mark W. Huddleston, insists that the

BFLG is not school policy. He also claims to be "troubled by many of the things in the language guide, especially the suggestion that the use of the term 'American' is misplace or offensive."

Whether Huddleston is sincere on this score, or whether he realized that the language guide released by the institution over which he presides is getting some bad press—the BFLG, he concedes, is "offensive to many, myself included"—is anyone's guess. However, given his subsequent comment that "the only NHU policy on speech is that it is free and unfettered on our campus," Huddleston sounds as self-delusional as the authors of the guide who see their work as an intellectual achievement.

"Universities are places to look at the world in new ways," they write in their introduction. "As a university organization, we care about the life of the mind."

As this little guide to "bias-free language" makes clear, this is self-delusion of epic grandeur.

Far from being "places to look at the world in *new ways,*" universities generally, and, evidently, the University of New Hampshire specifically, encourage students to look at the world in the same, *old*, unadventurous ways that they have imbibed from the larger culture, a Politically Correct, left-of-center culture for which most contemporary academics insist upon being apologists.

Maybe UNH really does "care" for "the life of the mind."

But it cares to dominate and control the minds of its students.

Jack Kerwick

"Safe Spaces" for Some Students, But Not Others

COLLEGE CAMPUSES IN contemporary America are rough places.

At any rate, it is of this that SJWs ("Social Justice Warriors"), i.e. "progressive" activists, have been assuring the country for quite some time.

"Racism," "sexism," "homophobia," "transphobia," "ageism," "ableism," "classism"—all of the "isms" and "phobias" that the left insists are endemic to Western civilization generally and America specifically have not only infected academia. To judge from the tireless rhetoric of both leftist student activists and their ideological ilk in the professoriate, these secular sins may be even more ensconced in colleges and universities than they are in the larger society.

"Hey, hey, ho, ho, Western civ has got to go!" Nearly 30 years ago, Jesse Jackson led hordes of students at Stanford University with this chant as they succeeded in pressuring the school to jettison required courses in Western civilization. The Western Civilization curriculum, so went the thinking at the time, is ridden with "European and Western male bias," biases that privilege white men over and against historically "marginalized" groups.

This line of thinking (or unthinking) dominates academia to the present day.

Higher Miseducation

To put it bluntly: Unless one is white, heterosexual, Christian, and deviates from the hegemon of Political Correctness (PC) that rules academia, the current climate on college campuses promises to be oppressive.

This is the version of reality advanced by SJWs. Reality itself, however, is quite otherwise.

In reality, it is true that college campuses have indeed become oppressive. The disinterested pursuit of truth and knowledge; the free marketplace of ideas; the cultivation of intellectual and moral virtues—these goods that have traditionally been the university's *raison d' etre* have largely given way to a new ideal: *activism.*

More exactly, today's faculty and students are preoccupied with activism on behalf of Social Justice. And anything or anyone that is perceived as a potential impediment to this end can't be tolerated. Social Justice by whichever means necessary!

College campuses *have* become oppressive places—but only for heterodox students and academics. In other words, those who dare to challenge academia's PC dogmas risk being ostracized, intimidated, and even threatened with violence.

Olivia Corn, a Cornell University student and the president of the school's Young Republicans, was assaulted the night after Donald J. Trump was elected to the presidency. While speaking to a couple different papers, Corn said:

> *I was actually assaulted on campus for being a Republican.*

She elaborated:

> *Out of nowhere I was on my phone and looking at my email and out of nowhere I felt two hands grab my shoulders and just sort of threw me to the ground, and they were yelling, 'F**k you, racist bitch, you support*

a racist party.

Before the election, Corn told the school newspaper that she would vote for Trump over Hillary Clinton. Subsequently, she received death threats.

Since she was attacked, she walks with an alarm at all times and refuses to walk alone on campus, especially after dark. This is "not something that I should have to be concerned with," Corn stated:

> *I'm a college student, I'm just trying to get good grades, get to law school, keep my head down—besides being the head of an organization.*

At St. Olaf College, Democrat students outnumber Republicans by at least four-to-one. The school paper interviewed 12 students who supported Trump. Nearly all of them confessed to feeling that a toxic campus atmosphere had rendered impossible civil, rational discourse with fellow students and professors over politically-oriented issues.

Emily Schaller, the President of the College Republicans, was threatened by another student on election night and called a "f**king moron." In the ensuing days, Schaller overheard groups of students talking loudly amongst themselves about "hurt[ing] the next conservative or Republican they saw."

Kathryn Hinderaker (gee, where are all of the feminists?), the Vice-President of the College Republicans, encountered the same phenomenon. She told her school paper that "one of the hardest things" occurred the day after the presidential election. It was at that time that, upon entering a campus building, she heard someone shout assurances to all Trump voters that they had "better be f**king scared!" To this, all who were present "clapped and applauded."

"Obviously," she concludes, "it didn't feel super safe."

Higher Miseducation

But it's not just *students* who are threatening Republicans and conservatives with violence.

At Cal State Fullerton, lecturer Eric Canin is said to have assaulted a Republican student when the latter and his peers counter-demonstrated against an anti-Trump demonstration led by the professor of cultural anthropology. Allegedly, Canin approached the students, asked if they had any faculty that were marching with them (they did not), and then said that only the "uneducated" would favor immigration restrictions, a wall, a travel ban, etc. He then lunged to grab at one of the counterdemonstrators' signs and pushed a couple of them.

Canin is presently suspended.

In January, at Georgetown University, several people claiming to belong to a group called "Refuse Fascism" burst into classrooms while classes were in session, distributed flyers, and denounced Trump and Vice President Mike Pence. The disrupters were also trespassers, for they were not Georgetown students.

Upon being removed from campus by security, many students admitted to being at once shocked and a bit shaken. One student told the school newspaper: "It is easy to feel like you are living in a secluded bubble on campus, and it is kind of scary that these random people made their way into my class."

In February, as most people now know, the University of California at Berkeley was engulfed by a full-scale riot courtesy of those of its students and faculty who objected to the presence of a speaker with whom they disagreed. The agents of intolerance attacked property and persons with bricks, fireworks and pepper spray in order to prevent those members of the community who were interested in doing so from hearing an alternative perspective.

While it isn't the case that all non-leftist college speaking events are accompanied by the dramatic displays of incivility and intolerance that's rampant at Berkeley, it is anything but uncommon for "conservative" speakers to meet with no small measure of hostility when visiting campuses. That this aggression is considerable is gotten easily enough from the fact that conservative speakers routinely require beefed-up security details.

For example, earlier this month, at Middlebury College, the social scientist, conservative-leaning Charles Murray was shouted down by unruly students and driven to deliver his speech from a secret, undisclosed location. A group of students stood up in the auditorium, turned their backs to Murray, and then spoke over him. One administrator who was present implored the disruptors to be respectful, to listen to and engage those perspectives to which they take exception—but to no avail. Other faculty members who attended the event lifted not a finger to calm the disturbance.

Those who mock the notion of college "safe spaces" are mistaken. Safe spaces are needed.

They are needed, though, for conservative and moderate students who dare to deviate from leftist groupthink.

Higher Miseducation

Caught on Video: Professor Tells Students to Break Laws, "Smash" System of "White Supremacy"

WHAT I HAVE frequently referred to as the Academic-Industrial-Complex (AIC) really is an organ of sorts of what I call the Racism-Industrial-Complex (RIC).

One of the more recent illustrations of this point is Albert Ponce, a professor of political science at Diablo Valley College. One of Ponce's lectures was recently video recorded by one of his students. The student released it to *The Red Elephants*—an on-line organization that has launched a campaign encouraging students to record their "Marxist professors—who in turn shared it with the campus watchdog publication, *Campus Reform.*

Ponce is captured on video assuring his students that since America's is a system of "white supremacy," the flag "is not really representative of everybody [.]"

"We are taught to get up and to pledge allegiance to the flag every single day." However, the "flag is not really representative of everybody who is standing up in that room. Maybe that's the way it should be taught. All those who this flag represents stand up, and maybe 50 percent of this room, *you remain seated because this is not for you*" (emphasis added).

To be fair, the Albert Ponces of the contemporary academic world are a dime-a-dozen. While the drivel that he espouses is obnoxious, and while it can't fail to jolt the sensibilities of many to see and hear a professor at a taxpayer-subsidized institution engage in educational malpractice by substituting anti-American *preaching* for *teaching* in the liberal arts, the tragic truth of the matter is that Ponce, in these respects, is indistinguishable from the vast majority of his colleagues in academia in these respects.

Nevertheless, it is good and just that this video is going viral, there has been a backlash, and that parents of current and prospective DVC students can discover for themselves the depths of the cesspool to which radical leftist academics have reduced our institutions of higher learning.

The United States Constitution, Ponce says, "should be called a white man's constitution."

So, the "white supremacy" that is America is in the proverbial DNA of the country. On this score, Ponce is unequivocal:

"And there were people here, the indigenous people, who were part—who paid a price, a very heavy price, for this project that is unfolding of white supremacy."

Ponce also labels the American system "white democracy." While supplying a slide presentation with this title, Ponce expresses his disdain toward President Trump and Attorney General Session: "So it is fitting that a white supremacist of old with a white supremacist of today exists and sit—they are smiling in the White House."

Yet the Ponce video is especially valuable insofar as it reveals the logic of his ideology, the inescapable implication of his conviction—to repeat, a conviction shared by the overwhelming majority of his colleagues—that America is a thoroughly oppressive place.

It isn't just that America is a "system" of "white supremacy," though it is, of course, this. Ponce insists that in addition to being "white supremacist," the American system is also "patriarchal, heteronormative, [and] capitalist [.]"

Thus, with a system so oppressive to women, gays, the transgendered, and nonwhites, there can be no negotiation. There can be no "reform."

There can only be "*abolition.*"

"What does abolition mean? Abolition means we must destroy it, not reform it. No voting is going to help. No writing your congressperson."

Ponce declares: "We need to *smash* white supremacy" (emphasis mine).

And *how* exactly does Ponce propose "the oppressed" go about "smashing" "white supremacy"? His answer is blunt:

Laws must be violated.

Those who "write" the law—the "oppressors"—have "convince[d] all of us to follow it," Ponce asserts. Yet "you shouldn't," he continues, for "the laws existing," at least "many" of them, "we should be violating [.]"

This is activism, radical leftist activism. This is not teaching. To put it another way, Ponce represents as clearly as anyone the prevailing impulse among academics to forego the *education* of their students in favor of *training* them in the ideology of their instructors, an ideology that entails relentless activism against the very civilization that both birthed the institutions of higher learning of which these students and their professors avail themselves as well as bestowed upon them every other privilege and blessing.

Why would any parent who is remotely concerned with the intellectual and moral well-being of his or her children pay big bucks to place them at the mercies of academics, like Professor Ponce, who despise the institutions, traditions, and, by implication, most of the people of the West and America?

How can taxpayers sit idly by why their hard-earned dollars are siphoned off by bureaucrats and channeled to subsidize the rantings of the Albert Ponces?

To be sure, the ideal of a liberal arts education remains a beautiful one. And there remain talented, capable, and dedicated academics—some of whom are on the liberal-left—who labor diligently to realize that ideal for themselves and, importantly, their students. Regrettably, though, they are in the minority, outflanked on all sides by folks like Albert Ponce.

Besides the fact that Ponce deprived students of the education to which they are entitled, there is another tragedy in all of this.

Ponce and his far-left, activist colleagues are, in a very real sense, the victims of their own ideology. Blinded, they fail to recognize that the conceptual resources that they draw upon to condemn "white supremacy" and all of the rest *are* the *self-same* moral ideas that distinguish from all others the civilization that they condemn as "white supremacist," "sexist," "homophobic," etc.

Most saliently, these anti-American, anti-Western professors presuppose the truth of the distinctively—no, the *uniquely*—Western, Christian concept of the Individual, for only if *the person* assumes moral importance over considerations of race, gender, sexual orientation, class, and so forth can it be immoral to regard people in terms of these ostensibly morally irrelevant categories.

Notably, these anti-American, anti-Western professors organize their worldview around their readings of Karl Marx, who Ponce refers to as "one of the most profound thinkers in the history of Western philosophy." Yet Marx was a 19th century German white man who was every bit as much a product of the "white supremacist" civilization against which 21st century "oppressed" professor rails.

It isn't only the students of these activist professors who are in need of a genuine education. The professors themselves need it just as badly.

Higher Miseducation

The Myth of a System of "White Supremacy"

LAST WEEK, JOHNNY Eric Williams, a professor of sociology at Trinity College, gained national notoriety.

Williams, who is black, posted some racially incendiary remarks on his Facebook wall. They were conjoined with the hashtag, "LetThemFuckingDie."

The hashtag Williams borrowed from an article published at *The Medium* and written in response to the recent mass shooting of Republican congressmen in Alexandria, Virginia. The essay's author, "Son of Baldwin," expressed regret that a black police officer risked her life to save the lives of "white bigots" and urged other blacks who are in positions to do the same to refrain from indulging the impulse.

Instead, they should:

"Let.Them.Fucking.Die."

The backlash against Williams and his employer was massive and sudden. Two Connecticut congressmen, Trinity College alumni, issued a statement imploring Trinity to terminate Williams immediately. Supposedly, the now infamous professor went into hiding because of death threats that he received.

Williams and his supporters among Trinity faculty and students insist that he meant to call for the death of, not white *people,* but "*a system* of *white supremacy.*"

"White supremacy" and like terms have ominous connotations associated with them; everyone knows that they are really, really bad. However, when push comes to shove, they prove awfully difficult to define. In fact, few people, least of all those who constantly invoke these terms, even bother to try to define them

The truth is, when it comes to charges of "white supremacy," "racism," and so forth, the Johnny Williams of the world would prefer to avoid doing the hard work of defining, or trying to define, their terms of choice. This is because it is infinitely easier for them to continually move the proverbial goalpost so as to satisfy their political needs of the moment.

The great 18th century philosopher David Hume made this point: "It is easy for a false hypothesis to maintain some appearance of truth, while it keeps wholly in generals" and "makes use of undefined terms [.]" Hume also said that "ideas, especially abstract ones, are naturally faint and obscure: the mind has but a slender hold of them: they are apt to be confounded with other resembling ideas; and when we have often employed any term, though without a distinct meaning, we are apt to imagine it has a determinate idea annexed to it."

"Systems of white supremacy," "institutional racism," and "white privilege" are abstractions. They are valued and tirelessly trotted out precisely because they are abstractions. The truth is that concrete individual white "racists," i.e. those who harass, intimidate, and attack blacks, simply aren't in large enough supply to sustain the narrative of perpetual White-on-Black-Oppression that is the lifeblood of the Racism-Industrial-Complex (RIC).

Indeed, flesh and blood white "racists" or "supremacists" are all too rare. The proof of this is not only in the data—which shows that, overwhelmingly, blacks tend to be perpetrators of interracial attacks while whites are just as overwhelmingly the victims—but in three other facts.

That RIC sales agents long ago shifted their focus from individual and overt "racism" to "covert," "subconscious," and/or "institutional racism"; regularly trade in hoaxes; and continually make "honorary whites" of those people of color who have had altercations with black criminal suspects (who these same RIC merchants then elevate into national martyrs) definitively establish the scarcity of real-life "white supremacists."

These considerations also prove that RIC agents *know* that there is a scarcity of "white supremacists."

Thus, it is this reality and this knowledge of the reality that gives rise to the need on the part of those who depend on keeping the Big Lie alive to retreat from the real world and take refuge behind abstractions like "systems of white supremacy."

It is a strange system of "white supremacy" that, for over 50 years, has restricted immigration to America from European, i.e. white, countries while encouraging relentless immigration from non-white ones.

It is a strange system of "white supremacy" that, annually, attracts millions of non-white peoples to leave their homelands, risking life and limb, to come and live under it.

It is a strange system of "white supremacy" to which African blacks fled, voluntarily, in greater numbers over a mere 15 year period (1990-2005) than were brought to America as slaves.

It is a strange system of "white supremacy" that makes it possible for its black citizens to live at a standard of living not only higher than that at which blacks live anywhere else in the world, *especially* in Africa, but a standard of living higher than that at which *whites* live in other parts of the world.

It is a strange system of "white supremacy" that has expended *trillions* of dollars since the 1960s on countless social programs aimed at *combatting* "white supremacy" or "racism" and uplifting blacks.

It is a strange system of "white supremacy" that spawns numerous race-based preferential treatment policies ("affirmative action," "diversity," etc.) meant to privilege blacks over their white counterparts.

It is a strange system of "white supremacy" whose architects allow for the election and re-election to office of the Presidency of, not just a black man, but a black man with an Arabic-sounding name.

It is a strange system of "white supremacy" that allows for blacks to occupy such powerful and nation-shaping positions as those of Supreme Court Justice, Attorney General, National Security Adviser, Secretary of State, and Chairman of the Joint Chiefs of Staff.

It is a strange system of "white supremacy" that allows blacks (and other nonwhites) to become multimillionaires and celebrities as athletes, entertainers, media personalities, politicians, and in business.

It is a strange system of "white supremacy" under which Nigerians in America have a higher annual household income than do whites.

It is a strange system of "white supremacy" under which Asians, i.e. nonwhites, earn more than every other ethnic group. Asians in "white supremacist" America also have lower rates of criminality, illegitimacy, drug use, unemployment, and suicide than every other group—including whites.

What a strange system of "white supremacy" this is!

I could continue in this same repetitive vein. The case, I believe, has been made amply:

There is no system of white supremacy.

However, Johnny Williams and his ilk must insist that there is, for they are race pimps, forever sucking at the nipple of the Racism-Industrial-Complex.

Professor Declares "Whiteness" a Disease

I HAD ALWAYS looked upon my six year old son as a blessing.

But now I realize that he is a *disease*.

So too is my wife, my parents, my grandparents, and every member of my family, both living and deceased, a disease.

But if you are reading this right now, and you are white, you should know that so are your children, and all of your loved ones, a disease.

So implies a University of Colorado education professor, Cherly E. Matias, in the most recent edition of *Teaching Education*, a peer-reviewed journal.

In "'Why Do You Make Me Hate Myself?': Re-teaching Whiteness, Abuse, and Love in Urban Teaching Education," the author insists that "the racial achievement gap" and other racial disparities are "symptoms" of "the underlying *diseases* of Whiteness and racism" (italics added).

Whiteness is a disease.

Matias explains that while the "inclusion of socially just philosophies in the curriculum is indeed essential" in order "to meet the needs of a growing urban populace," such philosophies "can mask the recycling of normalized, oppressive Whiteness."

Thus, it is imperative, Matias maintains, to "deconstruct Whiteness, abuse, and love in teacher education."

The problem, Matias assures us, is that by "denying race

during white childhood via a color-blind ideology," whites leave "lasting emotional scars, impressions that perpetuate the institutional silencing of race in teacher education." Urban students of color are made to "endure a racist educational system and daily racial battle fatigue."

But the difference between this "racism" and that faced by students and other "people of color" in the past is that the former is "color blind racism [.]"

The author maintains that "until teacher education programs make *confronting and exploring Whiteness a priority*, they cannot *truly love* their urban students of color as *complete beings* and so *deny humanity* full and just consideration" (italics added).

Whiteness is a disease.

And it is a disease that whites spread through their embrace of....color-blindness.

Let this sink in.

Matias is hardly an anomaly in today's academy. In fact, her thought is quite typical of the hard left zeitgeist that passes for enlightened thinking among liberal arts and humanities professors at institutions of "higher learning" all over the country (and beyond).

Matias draws on what's known as "critical race theory" (CRT). Given the heavily politicized nature of the contemporary academy, it should come as no surprise that CRT is a racialized version of Marxism *and* all of the rage among legions of academics.

Just as Marx and Engels sought to supply a comprehensive vision—an ideology—of the world by explaining (or explaining *away*) all of history and culture in terms of impersonal economic processes and the relations of "power" that they generate, proponents of CRT as well endorse a similar form of reductionism.

Only here, it is primarily *race* that serves as the "substructure" of society, and while economics continues to play a vital role in determining asymmetries of "power" between social groups, race and "racism" are the determining factors.

As such proponents of CRT as Richard Delgado and Jean Stefanic inform us in the introduction to their *Critical Race Theory: An Introduction,* CRT differs from more "traditional civil rights" approaches inasmuch as it "questions the very foundations of a liberal order, including equality theory, legal reasoning, Enlightenment rationalism, and neutral principles of constitutional law."

To put it more exactly, CRT holds that "racism is ordinary, not aberrational [.]" It is "the usual way that society does business, the common, everyday experience of most people of color in this country." Moreover, "racism" serves the "material" and "psychic" interests of both "white elites" and "working class whites."

"Racism" is *omnipresent.*

Yet it is omnipresent not in the sense that all white *individuals* are *consciously* "racist;" "racism" is omnipresent in the sense that it is *systemic* and, hence, largely *unconscious.*

Another especially noteworthy respect in which CRT reveals both its Marxian impress and its political character is its emphasis on "activism." Delgado and Tranfic are blunt in expressing their interest in "studying and transforming the relationship among race, racism, and power."

To repeat what was said above, both parents of college-bound children and taxpayers should know that the Cheryl Matiases and Richard Delgados of the world are not only well-represented in academia; their thought *saturates* the liberal arts and humanities.

It should also be clear by now that, by design, CRT (not unlike every other department that has been invented for the sake of advancing gender and racial identity politics) is self-immunized against the very possibility of refutation. And this is because it is meant to *preempt* argument. Consider: If whites think *as whites* or *collectively*, then they are guilty of "racism." Yet so too are whites "racist" if they insist upon judging people by the content of their character, not the color of their skin, i.e. if they endorse a "color blind ideology."

No matter what, the game is rigged in advance to convict all whites of "racism."

Proponents of CRT, in their singular (obsessive) focus upon distributions of "power," betray their end game: It is *they* who seek power. In fact, they seek a *monopoly* on power.

This is the objective of all who rely upon "Newspeak." The great philosopher Roger Scruton explains: "Newspeak occurs whenever the main purpose of language—which is to describe reality—is replaced by the rival purpose of asserting power over it."

While Newspeak "sentences sound like assertions," the truth is that "their underlying logic is the logic of the spell." Newspeak is talismanic, not persuasive. Its language is meant to blind us to what's right in front of our faces, to render us oblivious to reality.

Scruton quotes Francoise Thom, who observed that communists used Newspeak "to protect ideology from the malicious attacks of real things." Ditto with CRT.

Newspeak is notable, Scruton remarks, for its…

> …*use of nominalizations instead of direct verbs, the lack of indexicals, the preference for the passive voice and impersonal idioms, the replacement of predications with comparatives, the ubiquitous imperative mood.*

In other words, Newspeak trades in impersonal, highly general abstractions, i.e. "isms." Critical Race Theory is a textbook illustration of this: The individual is swallowed up, his or her intentions dissolved before the omnipresence of "*systemic racism.*"

Higher Miseducation

It is with this, parents, that your children are being inundated. Dear taxpayer, it is for the sake of subsidizing this anti-intellectual drivel that you labor.

But let's get even more exact: White parents and taxpayers are paying the salaries of faculty and administrators so that the latter can turn around and declare to the next generation that they are a "disease."

Jack Kerwick

A Professor and the Double Standards of Academia

GEORGE YANCY, AN Emory University philosophy professor and author of such books as *Look, a White!* recently wrote a *New York Times* op-ed. In "I Am a Dangerous Professor," Yancy, who is now on a "Professor Watchlist," in effect complains that to the burden of having been born black he now has *this* stigma with which to contend.

Professor Watchlists are forms of Orwellian "Newspeak" designed to contract, rather than expand, thought, Yancy informs us. They constitute a form of "McCarthyism" that is "consistent with a nostalgic desire 'to make America great again'" and motivated by a desire to "expose and oppose those voices in academia that are anti-Republican or express anti-Republican values."

The Professor Watchlist on which Yancy finds himself "is a form of exposure designed to mark, shame and silence." It isn't just that it encourages others to "spy" on leftist professors. It is also meant to "install forms of psychological self-policing to eliminate thoughts, pedagogical approaches and theoretical orientations that it defines as subversive."

The Watchlist is intended to stigmatize as "un-American" those, like Yancy, whose "ideas," "desires," and "passion" are all oriented toward "undo[ing] injustice [.]" Yancy laments that he had "been marked enough—as bestial, as criminal, as inferior—

just for being "a black man [.]" But now, in addition to this "racialized scarlet letter," he must reckon with this new threat against his person that is contrived to "adjust" him "philosophically" and "pedagogically."

Yancy defiantly declares that rather than "run in shame," as the drafters of the Watchlist would (allegedly) prefer, he instead experienced "a feeling of righteous indignation, even anger." The latter, Yancy tells us, "functions as a saving grace, a place of being" that frustrates the aims of the authors of the Professor Watchlist who "would rather I become numb, afraid and silent." Yancy warns: "If we are not careful, a watchlist like this can have the impact of…a theoretical prison designed to create a form of self-censorship among those imprisoned."

But Yancy will not be silenced. He will continue practicing what he calls "high stakes philosophy," a pedagogical approach aimed at making his students "maladjusted and profoundly unhappy with the world as it is." This "form of practicing philosophy…refuses to ignore the horrible realities of people who suffer [.]"

Yancy wants for his students "to lose sleep over the pain and suffering of so many lives that many of us deem disposable. I want them to become conceptually unhinged, to leave my classes discontented and maladjusted."

And what are "the horrible realities" of which Yancy "refuse[s] to be silent" in his classroom? They are: "racism, its subtle systemic structure;" "patriarchal and sexist hegemony and the denigration of women's bodies;" "forms of militarism in which innocent civilians are murdered in the name of 'democracy'"; "the existential and psychic dread and chaos experienced by those who are targets of xenophobia and homophobia;" violence against "transgender women and men;" the murder of "unarmed black bodies" by "the state and its proxies;" the ridicule and dehumanization of "those with disabilities;" and the "suffer[ing]" that we visit upon the planet.

Yancy concludes: "Well, if it is dangerous to teach my students to love their neighbors, to think and rethink constructively and ethically about who their neighbors are, and how they have been taught to see themselves as disconnected and neoliberal subjects, then, yes, I am dangerous and what I teach is dangerous."

This op-ed is telling for a variety of reasons.

First, as is obvious and all too expected of far too many black academics in the liberal arts, Yancy relishes in an acute sense of his own victimhood. It is precisely by virtue of assuming the role of the perpetually oppressed black victim in our culture's Politically Correct passion narrative that Yancy has been able to achieve his professional fortunes.

However, in reality, as a tenured professor at an elite institution like Emory University who has succeeded in making a living by exploiting an accident of birth while demonizing as "racist" and the like the white majority that he supposedly fears, Yancy is anything but a victim.

He is among the most privileged of human beings of any race.

Second, the only "horrible realities" to which Yancy refers are those that he sees through the prism of his far left ideology. The only suffering with which he can empathize is limited to that of those to whom this ideology allocates full personhood. As to the suffering of the Other—whites, white men, white heterosexual men—Yancy is of a piece with his ilk in being not indifferent, but utterly insensitive, and even cruel. Such expressions of suffering he attributes to the most malevolent of motives: "racism," "sexism," "homophobia," and every other "ism" and "phobia" in the left's inventory of unpardonable transgressions.

Third, neither Yancy nor any other faculty member virtually anywhere who shares his ideological stripes has a single reason to fear professional repercussions for the views that they espouse. Yancy's list of grievances with his ideological conception of reality is exactly that of the overwhelming majority of his fellow academics in humanities and liberal arts departments in most institutions of higher learning around the country.

And since there is nothing for a left-wing professor, particularly a black left-wing professor, to fear in spouting the academy's orthodoxy, *there is no courage* in doing so.

In fact, there is a profound lack of courage in peddling "Groupthink," another Orwellian term that, unsurprisingly, Yancy chooses not to quote.

Finally, though it is not my way, in the spirit of the standard operating procedure of the Yancys of the world, I too will be a bit autobiographical—egocentric—here.

Professor Yancy speaks about the "righteous indignation, even anger" that prevents him from being silenced. Well, I feel that anger too. I feel it intensely. And I feel it toward the likes of Professor Yancy, PC academics whose plush and often tenured existences are typically accompanied by an attachment to fashionable dogmas and a moral exhibitionism that is as excessive as is these academics' intolerance of those who dare to challenge those dogmas.

I am angry as hell, even outraged, by the self-pity of entitled leftist academics, especially black and minority professors, like Yancy, bullies who control the universities by branding as moral inferiors deserving of social death those academic dissidents who defy the reigning hegemony of ideas of which Yancy and his ilk are self-appointed guardians.

I am angry, *bitter,* that Yancy and the legions of academics that he represents seek either to harm or neglect altogether the professional prospects of untenured academics that, being white, male, heterosexual, Christian, and conservative, do not belong to any of their politically-protected classes.

I am enraged that the Yancys of the contemporary academy

preach for the need to appreciate the suffering of others while they are indifferent or even resentful toward the immeasurable agony of countless numbers of whites (and others) whose lives have been forever shattered by the brutality of their black victimizers. I'd be willing to bet Professor Yancy his job that he's never empathized with Channon Christian, Christopher Newsom, Brad Heyka, Heather Muller, Aaron Sandler, Jason Befort, and "Holly G." He's never urged his students to lose sleep over these white victims of black violence. He hasn't sought to make them "unhinged" by asking them to imagine themselves in the place of the loved ones of these victims.

And these constitute just a tiny fraction of the names of those whose fate has been to succumb to their black tormentors (and if Yancy thinks that I am being hyperbolic here, I can easily arrange for him to receive *daily* links, *multiple* times a day, to stories and *videos* of the phenomena of black-on-non-black violence).

Like Yancy, I too am a professor of philosophy. Unlike him, I am not tenured at an elite university. Unlike Yancy, before I was hired full-time three years ago, I spent 14 years teaching at a variety of institutions every semester as an adjunct instructor.

Unlike Yancy, I don't endear myself to fellow academics by way of the things that I write. Moreover, because I am a dissident, a dissenter from the status quo that Yancy defends, I do have much to fear—every time I dare to play David to Yancy's Goliath.

Higher Miseducation

Academia's New Mission: Dismantling Whiteness

SOME RECENT EXAMPLES from the world of Higher Education make the point that I've been at pains to impress upon readers, namely that for as sprawling as is the Academic-Industrial-Complex (AIC), it is essentially a function of an even more expansive Racism-Industrial-Complex (RIC).

As an example, there's Brooklyn College's Laurie Rubel, professor of math education. According to the student journalists who run the college watchdog publication *Campus Reform,* Rubel wrote an article for the *Journal of Urban Mathematics Education* in which she contends that the concepts of "meritocracy" and "color-blindness" are both "tool(s) of whiteness."

The problem with meritocracy, Rubel asserts, is that it:

> ...ignores systemic barriers and institutional structures that prevent opportunity and success.

As for color-blindness, Rubel remarks:

> *Teachers who claim color-blindness—that is, they claim not to notice the race of their students—are, in effect, refusing to acknowledge the impact of enduring racial stratification on students and their families.*

Jack Kerwick

Rubel continues:

> *By claiming not to notice, the teacher is saying that she is dismissing one of the most salient features of the child's identity and that she does not account for it in her curricular planning and instruction.*

So, by aspiring to know and evaluate their students independently of their racial backgrounds, teachers promote "whiteness."

However, Rubel also contends that if teachers *notice* the racial backgrounds of their students, they're guilty of promoting "whiteness." For example, when teachers say of their students that they "can't relate" to them, they note differences. But, Rubel laments, these "differences are typically cast in terms of deficit constructions about students, their places, and their families."

In order to walk this tightrope, Rubel proposes that teachers include "social justice" issues into their math lessons.

Yet even when these issues have been incorporated, Rubel warns that "teaching for social justice" can be used as "a tool of whiteness" as long as teachers cling to the "belief that effort is always rewarded," a belief, like the beliefs in meritocracy and color-blindness, that coincides with "various tools of whiteness [.]"

It must be observed that Rubel's view is commonplace in the contemporary academy. Nor is it rare in her specific field, for just a couple of months ago, another mathematics education professor, Rochelle Gutierrez, argued essentially the same exact point. Only Gutierrez insisted that mathematics promoted "whiteness."

These are some of the titles featured in the most recent edition of *Journal of Urban Mathematics Education:*

Higher Miseducation

Beyond White Privilege: Toward White Supremacy and Settler Colonialism in Mathematics Education

'It's Influence Taints All': Urban Mathematics Teachers Resisting Performativity [concern with grades] through Engagements with the Past

Equity-Directed Instructional Practices: Beyond the Dominant Perspective

Math is More Than Numbers: Examining Beginning Bilingual Teachers' Mathematics Teaching Practices and Their Opportunities to Learn

There is also included a book review with the title:

Viewing 'Others' as Mathematicians

The book reviewed is called:

Inventing the Mathematician: Gender, Race, and Our Cultural Understanding of Mathematics

Over at the University of Iowa, Professors C. Kyle Rudick and Kathryn B. Golsan maintain in an academic paper that inasmuch as teachers aspire to insure *civility* in their classrooms, they "reproduce white racial power."

The alleged problem with what Rudick and Golsan refer to as "whiteness-informed civility" is that it "functions to assert control of space" and "create a good white identity."

In other words, "civility within higher education is a racialized, rather than universal, norm."

Rudick and Golsan interviewed ten white college students and asked them the following two questions:

Jack Kerwick

(1) What do you consider to be civil behavior?

(2) How do you think your racial identity may affect your understandings of civility when talking with students of color?

As should come as no surprise to anyone who has been paying any attention to today's academia, these students were damned if they did, damned if they didn't.

"First, participants stated that they tried to avoid talking about race or racism with students of color to minimize the chance that they would say something 'wrong' and be labeled a racist." Yet they also "described how they tried to be civil when interacting with students of color" by trying "to be overly nice or polite."

Either way, these white students, the researchers conclude, sustain "white privilege" and "white racial power."

Color-blindness, treating everyone the same regardless of race, is a "race-evasive" approach that "functions to erase racial identity in the attempt to impose a race-evasive frame on race-talk."

It is imperative for teachers to end this situation "by ensuring that White students and students of color engage in sustained, sensitive, and substantive conversations about race and racism." Faculty must "encourage White students to understand how using WIC [White Informed Civility] to downplay issues of race or racism in higher education serves to elide their own social location and reinforce the hegemony of White institutional presence."

Another University of Iowa education professor, Jodi Linley, wrote in a journal essay that her goal in the classroom is to "dismantle whiteness in my curriculum, assignments, and pedagogy."

Linley says:

> *For white students, talking about race with an all-white group of peers facilitates their realization that they are raced beings, thus revealing their own white ignorance.*

Linley tells us that her "teaching paradigm" is informed by her "identities" as a white person, yes, but also as "a queer, able-bodied, cisgender woman."

Professor Linley committed a few years back to "develop courses that both unveiled and rejected" the notion that "neutrality and objectivity are realistic and attainable." The problem with supposing that curricula can be neutral is that such a supposition facilitates "hegemonic racism, sexism, classism, ableism, cisgenderism, and heterosexism."

Linley "challenges" her students' "privilege" and engages in what she calls "interrupting oppression" in her classroom. She also practices racial segregation. The latter, according to *Campus Reform's* report on Professor Linley, supposedly contributes to fruitful exchanges between students on the role of "privilege" in their lives.

Unless they reckon with their "white privilege," Linley wants for her students to know, they will be "complicit" in the spread and strengthening of "white supremacy."

As these three illustrations—drops in an endless ocean of episodes to which I could have easily alluded—prove, the Academic-Industrial-Complex is an agent of the Racism-Industrial-Complex.

These examples prove this by showing not just that college curricula have been taken over by racial politics, but by showing that the discourse has been rigged from the outset to convict whites and white men specifically of "racism," irrespectively of how they conduct themselves.

Jack Kerwick

Conclusion

AS THESE CHAPTERS make painfully clear, the classical ideal of a liberal arts education—and along with it, reason and its concomitants, knowledge and truth—is under attack. This lamentable condition of academia notwithstanding, as an academic dissident who has spent the better part of the last two decades teaching philosophy, the subject that I love, and who remains equally in love with this beleaguered ideal, I choose to believe that while reason may be down, it is not yet out for the count. And she just may triumph before it is over.

My faith is not blind:

Exactly because the attack against reason has reached a fever pitch, it has elicited quite a backlash. There are now several campus watchdog organizations as well as an ever-burgeoning crop of academics—including, notably, liberal-left academics—who are laboring inexhaustibly to call attention to, and push back upon, the hard left's irrational excesses. Networks of like-minded academics, dissidents who are devoted to educating students into their civilizational inheritance, as opposed to indoctrinating them into a political creed, are developing and expanding.

The chances that the public will at long last be informed of the anti-Western politicization of the academy have never been greater.

Academic dissidents must continue to teach, and teach

passionately, in their fields. They must teach with an eye toward instilling in their students both understanding of and appreciation for the Euro-Christian or Western civilization that gave us the university and the ideal of liberal learning that the university was invented to promote.

Academic dissidents should spare no occasion to inform the public of the war against reason that has long been waged within academia.

Finally, the most effective way for dissidents to tackle reason's enemies is to do essentially what I attempted to do here: Expose them. Expose their claims. Do not *argue* with them. That the despisers of reason aren't interested in genuine argument, that they *cannot* be interested in genuine argument, should be obvious given their abandonment of reason.

If one insists upon arguing with reason's detractors, in order, say, to expose the incoherence, the contradictions, of their views, then so be it. At the very least, the academic dissident should never argue *defensively*. The dissident cannot permit himself to be roped into what reason's repudiators can only view as a game.

The academic dissident has no option but to continue soldiering onward. He requires the virtue of resilience, certainly. Yet, no less essential to his struggle, is the virtue of *hope*.

www.ingramcontent.com/pod-product-compliance
Lightning Source LLC
Chambersburg PA
CBHW022106040426
42451CB00007B/148